LIVING WITH CANCER: A TEEN PERSPECTIVE

LIVING WITH CANCER: A TEEN PERSPECTIVE

A Collection of Essays from the Gilda's Club New York City Essay Contest

GILDA'S CLUB NEW YORK CITY

EDITED BY TONYA HURLEY

WITH A FOREWORD BY EMMA STONE

Living with Cancer-A Teen Perspective: *A Collection of Essays From the Gilda's Club New York City Essay Contest*

ISBN: 1508700184
ISBN 13: 9781508700180

Inquiries concerning rights should be addressed to:
William Morris Endeavor Entertainment LLC
Attn: 212 Books
1325 Avenue of the Americas
New York, New York 10019
212books@wmeentertainment.com

CONTENTS

A Note From Gilda's Club CEO, Lily Safani· · · · · · · · · · · · ·vii
A Note From The Editor, Tonya Hurley · · · · · · · · · · · · · · · ix
A Special Note From Gilda's Club NYC Ambassador,
Emma Stone · xi

Part 1 About Me · 1
Chapter 1   Strength In Normalcy   By Jodi Ahn-Ting Chan· · · · · · · · · 3
Chapter 2   A Relay For My Life   By Molly Prep· · · · · · · · · · · · · · 7
Chapter 3   A Different Route   By Jamison Buchanan · · · · · · · · · · 9
Chapter 4   Dreams Deferred   By Dana N. Laurie · · · · · · · · · · · · ·14
Chapter 5   A Suburban Life   By Andrea Baatz· · · · · · · · · · · · · ·17
Chapter 6   The Broccoli Rabe Blog Story   By Donna Coane · · · · · · · ·23
Chapter 7   Cancer... Cancer   By Samantha Ashburn · · · · · · · · · · ·27
Chapter 8   Life Is A Journey, Not A Destination   By Saul Tbeile· · · · ·32
Chapter 9   Me And My Leukemia   By Mallory Evans · · · · · · · · · · · 36
Chapter 10 Cancer Kickoff   By Kalyn Faller· · · · · · · · · · · · · · · 40

Part 2 My Parents· ·45
Chapter 11 A Soft Blow   By Kayla Halvey · · · · · · · · · · · · · · · ·47
Chapter 12 Aloha Mahuakine: A Story In Pictures   By Emma Burger · ·53

Chapter 13 An Inspiration To Us All   By Jared May · · · · · · · · · · · · · · · 66

Chapter 14 It Was Something   By Joy Chiang Ling · · · · · · · · · · · · · · ·69

Chapter 15 My Greatest Accomplishment   By Chelsea De Jesus · · · · · · ·74

Chapter 16 Untitled   By Kenneth Hicks ·76

Chapter 17 Our New Lives With Cancer   By Saloni Vishwakarma · · · · ·79

Chapter 18 On The Sidelines   By Nina Leeds · · · · · · · · · · · · · · · · · · ·82

Part 3 Brothers, Sisters, And Bffs ·85

Chapter 19 The Sibling Story   By Sophia Capellini · · · · · · · · · · · · · ·87

Chapter 20 The Strongest Mother   By Erica Galluscio · · · · · · · · · · · · ·91

Chapter 21 One Dreadful Thing   By Alicia Romeo · · · · · · · · · · · · · · 97

Chapter 22 The Contradictions Of Cancer   By Emily Marcus · · · · · · · 99

Chapter 23 The Unbreakable Bond   By Bryce Cammarata · · · · · · · · · ·103

Chapter 24 The Ripple Effect   By Marcus Thomas · · · · · · · · · · · · · · ·106

Chapter 25 Indelible   By Annie Fan ·110

Part 4 My Family ·113

Chapter 26 Nana   By Emily Friedman ·115

Chapter 27 A Yellow Bracelet   By Caitlin Rubin · · · · · · · · · · · · · · · ·119

Chapter 28 Uncle Santa   By Rachel Rigodon · · · · · · · · · · · · · · · · · ·123

Chapter 29 Always In My Heart   By Ryan Markoe · · · · · · · · · · · · · · ·126

Chapter 30 Thank You   By Hannah Chi ·129

Chapter 31 The Emotional Rollercoaster   By Jack Bellear · · · · · · · · · ·131

Chapter 32 Diagnosis   By: Cassidy Latham · · · · · · · · · · · · · · · · · · ·139

A NOTE FROM GILDA'S CLUB
CEO, LILY SAFANI

A cancer diagnosis can be an extremely isolating experience that triggers many emotions, including fear, anger, depression and an overwhelming sense of helplessness. Gilda's Club New York City (GCNYC) is a non-profit dedicated to helping New Yorkers who have been impacted by a cancer diagnosis—men, women, teens and children—learn how to live with cancer. Our innovative program is an essential complement to medical care, providing networking and support groups, workshops, educational lectures and social activities, **all free of charge.** More important, we provide welcoming communities where people living with cancer, young and old, can share their experiences with others who understand what it means to be living with cancer. At Gilda's Club, we believe no one should face cancer alone.

The *"It's Always Something"* Teen Essay Contest was started in 2010 to provide a forum for teens in grades 9-12 to share their own personal cancer experience with other teens. A cancer diagnosis in the family is particularly hard on teens, who may have difficulty expressing their feelings and whose parents may not know how to talk to them. The essay contest provides them with an outlet to initiate a crucial dialogue about the impact of a cancer diagnosis in the family.

Through the generous support of the Heidi Paoli Fund, Gilda's Club NYC has now been able to publish selected essays from the *"It's Always Something"* Teen Essay Contest—a first for Gilda's Club NYC. This special publication of selected works from the 2010-2013 Teen Essay Contests provides teens with a forum to express themselves that many did not think was possible and helps to educate the public about the issues teens who are living with cancer face. We hope by publishing these essays other teens will understand that they do not have to face cancer alone.

Our annual *"It's Always Something"* Teen Essay Contest will continue to contribute to the mission of GCNYC and help identify teens who may benefit from our free cancer support program, Teens Connect, as well as educate a wider community about the benefit of social and emotional support for everyone living with cancer.

We could never accomplish what we do without the support of our special community of volunteers, donors and our Gilda's Club New York City staff. It is an endless list of people who truly believe in what we do and for whom we are forever grateful. Special thanks to our contributing teens, our judges, Dennis Paoli and the Heidi Paoli Foundation, Nancy Cambino, Michele Halusic, Tonya Hurley, Tracy Hurley Martin, William Morris Endeavor/212 Books, Kevin Dixon, Emma Stone and Migdalia Torres—all of whom have made the Teen Essay Contest what it is today.

Lily Safani
CEO
Gilda's Club New York City

A NOTE FROM THE EDITOR, TONYA HURLEY

I'd walked by Gilda's Club on Houston Street many times before, having worked in and around the neighborhood ever since I arrived in New York City from Pittsburgh. I was a fan of Gilda Radner and had admired the work that was being done in her name, but it wasn't until I had a cancer scare of my own that I actually entered its famously red door.

I had just given birth to my daughter Isabelle Rose when I found the lump. Soon, I was going through all kinds of biopsies and scans. It was a terrifying whirlwind filled with white, sterile rooms, painful tests, and strange faces. Oddly enough, I found myself thinking a lot about Gilda and what she went through. The first thing I did was order her book, "It's Always Something." I read it voraciously, relating to her in a way I never had before. Not just as a trailblazing, lovable comedian, but as a vulnerable human being. I relied on her during that time. I leaned on her. I took the book with me to my tests and read it while I waited. And waited. And worried. And waited. Eventually, I had to have surgery for a definitive answer. Even though I'd read the book a few times by then, I still took it with me to the hospital. A few weeks later, I was told that I didn't have cancer but another condition that puts me at high risk for developing cancer. I was so thankful that all I wanted to do was give back somehow.

So I headed for the red door.

Once inside, I felt right at home in a way I hadn't expected. I was able not only to see, but also to appreciate the hard work that Gilda's Club does to support those living with cancer and their families. All of it, for free. It was incredibly inspiring.

I met with the volunteer coordinator and told her how much I relied on Gilda's book while I was going through my ordeal. How much she had helped me—a friend that I'd never met, but somehow knew.

"I'm a young adult author," I explained. "What can I do to help?"

We began brainstorming. She told me that she was in the beginning stages of trying to organize a teen essay contest. My eyes lit up. I told her how I often encountered teen readers who'd been touched by cancer at book signings and events. *One of the first rules of writing is to write what you know,* I thought. *And, what better way for teens affected by cancer to express themselves?*

We talked about how great it would be if the teens could actually hear from their peers going through similar situations. So they could relate, feel comforted, and have someone to lean on during their journey. Something just like Gilda's book was for me. And so, the first Teen Essay Contest was born and the beginnings of this collection were launched.

Four years later, the first eBook was underway. With so many extraordinary essays to choose from, it was truly a daunting experience making these final selections. Our guiding spirit throughout this process was, of course, Gilda Radner, and the amazing fellow judges who signed on to help with such difficult yet rewarding decisions.

It has been an honor to be involved in such a life-affirming project. To witness in print the bravery and honesty of these teens. They've taught me so much about life, love and what it is to fight, to win, and sometimes to lose. Even as we make these accounts more widely available, I hope that the sense of intimacy and relatability that informs each of them shines through, allowing a few tears and lots of smiles. I hope that within these pages readers find a place to let go, to be themselves, and ultimately to find strength. That they find a writer here to relate to; to lean on.

That they find their Gilda.

A SPECIAL NOTE FROM GILDA'S CLUB

NYC AMBASSADOR, EMMA STONE

My mom was introduced to the comedy of Gilda Radner in her days on *SNL* when she was a teen in the 1970s. I was introduced to Gilda's comedy through my mom, and when I was a teen, my mom was diagnosed with breast cancer. Gilda's Club was founded on the same principles as The Wellness Community, the program that helped Gilda herself so much through her experience with cancer—a place to share and laugh and express feelings, whether you or a loved one are facing cancer, in order to heal.

With that in mind, the teen program at Gilda's Club provides an amazing outlet and support for teens that have been touched by cancer. These essays are a beautiful insight to the true and honest feelings that come up when you, a parent, or friend are affected by this disease. The teen program at Gilda's Club is so special and valuable, and these essays are brave examples of how important it is to share what's in your heart, in order to help yourself and others going through a similar experience. You are not alone!

PART 1

ABOUT ME

Chapter 1

STRENGTH IN NORMALCY

By Jodi Ahn-Ting Chan

It was 5:21 on a Saturday morning and I was awake. It wasn't for a job, or a tutoring program, or even because I couldn't sleep. It was because I had a sudden pain in my stomach that made me grip my bed sheets and run to the bathroom. Yes, this doesn't sound horrifying—an ordinary fifteen-year-old girl fleeing to the toilet because of a stomachache. But, there are two things wrong in this sentence: one, I wasn't an ordinary teenager, at least according to my doctors; and two, it wasn't a stomachache that made me vomit. It was chemotherapy.

I was in the seventh grade when I was first diagnosed with osteosarcoma, a complicated name for a simple concept: cancer. Before my diagnosis, cancer was a foreign thought to me; never did I concern myself about things like sickness, disease, sadness. One day, my parents noticed a large bump right under my right knee, a sort of circular shape the size of an orange. It hurt me to walk, but I never paid attention to it, thinking it was a bruise. My mother assumed the pain was a sign of me growing and I relished at the idea of being five foot two, a whole inch taller than my mother. My father thought it would go away, but after a few weeks, he saw it increase in size and took me to an acupuncturist. He massaged my knee and thwacked it with some sort of hammer.

Nothing worked. My mother grew worried and took me to my pediatrician, who suggested a supposedly well-known doctor at a hospital in Manhattan. Looking back, this was the decision that probably saved my life. This hospital was called Memorial Sloan-Kettering Cancer Center, a place that made itself a big name in the cancer treatment and research world. As all innocent and shielded little girls go, I was one of the most. Walking through the intimidating, ominous black sliding doors in the early morning gave me a sickly feeling; I knew before I was even X-rayed that this would be my home-away from home for a while.

The first doctor I saw was jovial and enthusiastically smiling. Her bright red hair matched her unique personality, as I soon grew to find. She welcomed us to the Pediatric Day Hospital, as if it was a special membership for select people. Another doctor was brought in, this time, he was much older, round with graying hair. They spent hours reviewing my health history and analyzing my X-rays. It was after five in the evening that they came back to me and my parents. It was almost six when the news finally registered in my mind and I started crying. It was a little past seven when I stopped crying alone and started crying with my parents.

In the next week, I had to say goodbye to all my middle school friends and teachers (a task so daunting itself that I broke out in tears each time), start chemotherapy, and prepare for a six-hour surgery. My life changed dramatically as I no longer was able to, well, live life. I was forced to go to the same generic hospital, sleep in the same white bed, eat the same bland foods, and breathe the same sanitized air; all without a random break scheduled in.

Because of all the toxic chemicals from chemotherapy, which killed both healthy and unhealthy cells, my stomach was always in knots, my shiny, smooth, black hair slowly fell off, and I was always exhausted. As needles were stuck into my arm and pills were swallowed, days and days passed as I followed the same routine. Waking up to throw up, getting dressed, falling asleep, getting shots, eating, throwing up, and sleeping. Each day blended with the one before it, and soon, the one after it. Mornings blurred into nights. Perhaps it was the medication or just the pain repression, but the year felt like it was only a week or two long.

After a month, I returned to school, only to stand out like a red cardinal in the winter snow. I felt like an outsider in the student body, the only person with wispy, thin hair, the only person walking with a metal cane, the only person with a scary scar from her knee to ankle, two raised scars on her chest, and a body swollen from the intravenous fluids. All my friends welcomed me back with open arms, but it was obvious from the sparse conversations and forced laughs that I didn't fit in anymore. I was a reflection of myself on the wrong side of the mirror and I didn't know it.

My remaining year of eighth grade consisted of awkward talks, constant limping back and forth from classrooms to the bus stop, and monthly doctor appointments, where I spent the whole day waiting, getting x-rayed, and being examined. The summer between my last middle school year and my freshmen year of high school was the three months that I finally felt closer to the "normal" I was before cancer. My hair was barely long enough to pass as a "fashion forward," boyish look that Emma Watson recently donned. And, more importantly, my limp was only noticeable if I walked quickly.

But it wasn't until the August before sophomore year that I was comfortable again in my own skin. By then, my hair grew long enough to reach my shoulders and tie into a ponytail. My weight had finally regulated and I barely limped anymore, even when I walked quickly and ran. I had a good group of friends that I spent almost every hour with and, to my surprise, I won my school's Student Government election and became the sophomore president. I was happy, popular, and... normal. It seemed as if the previous two years never happened. Until *it* came back into my life.

Only a month and a half after I assumed my role as class president and started my second year of high school, I was diagnosed with a relapse in osteosarcoma. A regular check-up lasted longer than usual and I ended up returning home waiting for a phone call. I couldn't eat or sleep or watch television. When my mother picked up the telephone, I knew what the doctor was saying on the other side and I ran upstairs to find my father intently staring at the computer screen. He looked up with sincere eyes and I ran to him. I sat in his lap like a child and cried. As tears fell from my eyes, he just held onto me and cried along. My father, the man who held pride in his ability to complete everything himself without help, the manliest man I knew, was crying.

From that day on, I knew it wasn't a question about whether or not I could do it again. It became a question about what I would do after I overcome this obstacle. I decided to take everything by its head. I had to give up my Student Government position. I had to restart home schooling. I shaved my head before my hair could fall out. I remembered each tile of the hospital and each picture on the walls. I knew each nurse's name and I greeted my doctors every morning. I feel like this bout passed faster than my first and I returned to school in the middle of junior year. Instead of the awkward reunions that I expected, I was met with genuine happiness and joy that I was back. I never realized how lucky I was to undergo chemotherapy twice and actually gain something from it; I realized that I was stronger than thought.

Strength isn't about your weight or the size of your muscles, it's how you take advantage of a situation and keep living. Perhaps surviving whatever is thrown my way is my secret strength. Also, I discovered that "normal" isn't actually quite normal. It differs for each person and my normal is being different and knowing that I always will be.

Chapter 2

A RELAY FOR MY LIFE

By Molly Prep

My school's Relay for Life last June was a coming-out of sorts for me. At age seven I was diagnosed with acute lymphoblastic leukemia. I underwent treatment for over three years. Even following those final sessions of chemo and being deemed cancer-free, my struggles left a muddy slew of emotions; an ache for childhood, a fear of relapse, and anger for the pain I'd caused my family. Determined not to let my illness define me, I bottled those murky feelings and told few of my experience.

Fast-forward to February of my junior year, when Relay for Life was announced in a moving school assembly. I was persuaded by my friends to join. Though hesitant at first, I eventually became a team co-captain. I was making progress in leaps and bounds, but still dreaded the event itself. I wondered whether or not I should wear the purple shirt that symbolized survivorship, or if I would emotionally be able to take part in events like the Survivor Lap. I didn't want my past sickness to identify me, for my classmates or teachers to stop seeing the person I really was.

Before I knew it, June 9th and Relay arrived. I busied myself getting things in order; anything to distract me from the looming decisions I wished to avoid. An announcement sounded: "Attention all Relayers: Please report to the track for opening ceremonies and laps." The time to choose had arrived. My team's chaperone, a teacher of mine who had survived breast cancer, held up her purple shirt and said, "I will if you will." How could I say no? Wearing our symbols of survival, we walked to the track and listened as speakers shared their stories of how cancer impacted their lives. I marveled at their composure and strength, and wondered if the same was possible for me. Then it was time for the Survivor Lap. I stepped onto the turf lanes, was handed a banner, and began to walk. I had worried that with that first step I'd cry, or scream, or collapse right in the middle of the track. I never imagined that I'd feel joy course through my veins. Walking with purple-clad survivors, I couldn't help but smile. I was alive. Although not everyone diagnosed with cancer has the same outcome, I knew that by participating in Relay for Life I was making a difference. My classmates ran up to me, stunned to discover my hidden past. They didn't realize that I was equally surprised with my newfound ability to say, "I survived cancer," not only without fear, but with pride. I felt liberated of my burden.

Walking the Survivor Lap was only the beginning. That night I went on to run ten miles. Forty laps; every step barefoot. I wanted to embrace such life with the wind in my hair, the sweat down my back, and the refreshing night air filling my lungs. The pounding of my exposed soles mimicked the mantra in my head: I'm alive. I'm alive. I'm *alive*.

It was only after the Relay grounds were cleared that I made the connection between the laps I ran and the leukemia I fought. The Survivor Lap didn't define my run that followed, but that first step did ignite something. Yes, my cancer shaped me, but it's far from the only thing that makes me who I am. Cancer was only one lap of my life; I still have many miles left in me to run.

Chapter 3

A DIFFERENT ROUTE

By Jamison Buchanan

My view on life has taken a much different route than most of my friends. Every morning was alike. I'd wake up with a headache, walk by the candle sitting on my dresser and get nauseated from the smell of it. I'd keep walking though, keep going and going; I never gave up. Sitting in my classroom in eighth grade Science, trying to put up with these headaches, was something I always dreaded. I was repeatedly told, by more than a few doctors, that I had a sinus infection that just "wasn't going away," and was prescribed more antibiotics after each course had ended. This occurred over and over. Finally entering my freshman year at high school, my mom and I realized none of this was the least bit normal. On January 1st, 2007, I didn't know where I lived, or even who my own mom was. My mom, suddenly aware of my drastic conditions, immediately drove me to Stamford Hospital, where both my parents were told I was pregnant because of the test results caused by hormone imbalances. I personally don't recall any of this because of the pressure in my head. My mom begged to differ, and forced the doctors to complete a cat-scan. Finally, after hours leading into the cat-scan, I was diagnosed with a mass on my brain and immediately rushed to Yale New Haven Hospital by ambulance.

As soon as we got to Yale, doctors explained to my mom that a stent, which is a drain, needed to be surgically placed through the skull to relieve pressure caused by fluid on my brain. My mom was told that without the stent, the excess fluid on my brain would have killed me. Fortunately, photographs are my only recollection of this experience. Later that month, after enough fluid had been relieved, a resection removed the tumor. The biopsy confirmed the tumor to be malignant. Afraid that she'd miss a doctor coming to discuss the results; my mom sat right next to me and never left the room once. This exemplifies my mom's endless devotion throughout the journey. My doctor confirmed that 99% of the golf ball-sized tumor had successfully been removed. From my point of view this was really great news, considering so many childhood tumors either can't be removed because of the location, or only a small percentage can be removed. On the other hand, the tumor had been lying against my pituitary and hypothalamus glands, which weren't so great. Before I was sick, I was not at all familiar with the pituitary or the hypothalamus glands whatsoever. I later learned that they are the most important glands of the body. They produce many hormones that travel in the body, and stimulate other glands to produce many more types of hormones. Because of the immense pressure against the two glands; I now suffer hypothyroidism and a complete hormonal imbalance. This causes a great deal of side effects including fatigue, lots of weight gain, weakness throughout the body, hot/cold intolerance, and more. Despite these difficult conditions, I refuse to give up. Even though my body and appearance has changed completely, I keep moving forward each day.

Shortly after my resection, the decision was made to surgically insert a port-o-cath, thus allowing chemo, blood transfusions and routine blood work easier on my body. I underwent four months of chemo at Yale–New Haven Hospital. As a result of my counts being low, my taste buds changed every day, muscles on my entire left side were weakened, traumatic experiences no one should ever have to deal with. I had to stay away from all the people I love, including my family and friends, just for the sake of not getting an infection.

Even a simple cold could be fatal to a cancer patient. I felt alienated, as if I were a stranger to those I love.

I could not have gotten through any of this without my mom by my side from day one. I believe her never-ending strength and spirit penetrated through me while I was sick. My mom taught me how to persevere through difficult times. She never gave up on me, and neither will I. My Child Life Specialists also really impacted my hospital experience in the most positive way. They always played Candyland and other games with me to try to keep my mind off "cancer". I hadn't realized it then, but these games were actually helping me regain my short-term memory skills. My child life specialists thoroughly explained every procedure that I underwent by illustrating on dolls and diagrams. They guided me every step of the way, as I continuously asked, and still do, "Why me?" They also supported my parents through every surgery I underwent. Many people do not realize how much cancer greatly affects the parents and siblings of an ill child. As a result of this experience, I am now determined to attend Wheelock College in Boston and become a Child Life Specialist. Because I have dealt with what ill children are going through "firsthand," I would like to "return the favor" that I received and help reduce their suffering by giving knowledgeable support to ill children and their families, and improve the wellbeing for all those who are affected by these debilitations and illnesses. I am the type of woman who sets a goal and meets it; I will never give up on what I set my mind to doing, and I believe that this is a huge strength, despite the adversity in my life.

Friends didn't give up on us either. They organized a dinner schedule for my entire family. Families in Darien voluntarily offered to deliver a home cooked meal to us every night. Dinner was always at our doorstep at a given time every evening, with a kind note along with it. These gifts of kindness made a huge difference, coming home after hours of chemo to a home cooked meal waiting at your door. Complete strangers became friends during this time.

In times of need, the true colors of people and organizations shine through. My radiation therapy, to remove the 1% of the tumor remaining in my brain, took place at Massachusetts General Hospital, in the summer of 2007. My mom and I had been chosen to stay at *Christopher's Haven* for the time of my treatment, which is an organization that provides housing for families of children undergoing cancer treatment. We were very lucky to be living in this apartment and we actually enjoyed walking all over Boston more than we had expected. The bond between my mother and me strongly developed. Even though I was living in Boston solely for cancer treatment, I really appreciated its surroundings and everything Boston had to offer. Luckily for us, we didn't even need a car because we walked to and from treatment, which was conveniently right across the street. My proton beam radiation was scheduled every day for 2 months. Having my music playing during treatment really helped me cope and relax through the lengthy procedure. After that, I usually had one hour of tutoring to keep me caught up in school. I never gave up my school work, or anything for that matter, while undergoing treatment. I achieved greatly despite the adversity throughout my illness.

All was going very well, and we finally heard the words we were waiting to hear, "100% cancer free...". On the other hand, the side of effects of chemo and all my medications continue. After radiation therapy, I noticed that I couldn't hear that well in my left ear. Once I saw an ear doctor, I learned that I lost 50% of my hearing in my left ear and 10% in my right ear. This made it extremely difficult to keep up in classes, when I could barely make out what the teacher or my peers were saying. I now have to have words repeated over and over again in order to conceptualize them properly. I also slowly began gaining weight, continuing for almost two years. Months went by as doctors continuously tried to figure out what was going on. I was then diagnosed with the lowest thyroid levels ever seen, causing all the weight gain and fatigue. I did everything from seeing a nutritionist, to working out at the gym every day. Although I was told that no matter how much I worked out and ate healthily, I would still gain weight, I still do these for the benefit of my body. Nonetheless, I persevere. Shortly after treatment ended, I signed up for a gym membership at the YMCA. Being bald at the time, people would often whisper or stare. I remember when a kid pointed at me and said, "Look, she's bald," and this made me feel very insecure. About a month later, an elderly man came up to me at the YMCA and said, *"You're beautiful just the way you are; don't let anybody tell you otherwise.*" It was from that moment on that I realized everything really does happen for a reason; and even if the journey is horrible, people like this make all the difference. It was a real epiphany.

On the other hand, just because you're cancer free doesn't at all mean you're done with the whole process. Because of cancer I'm currently more than double my size. And because of that I'm physically incapable to do crew, which I used to love, or hang out with my friends for more than a short period of time, let alone do a full day of school classes. Because of cancer, my life will always be completely different. I now have horrible stomach issues and headaches almost every day. As a result of all these problems, I started to get really far behind in eleventh grade due to all the doctor appointments and not feeling well enough to attend my classes. Thank God for the teachers who voluntarily stepped up to the plate to tutor me every day at home, helping me to successfully finish my junior year of high school. Again, it was all these little things that added up along the way, making the biggest difference in the world.

No one ever wants to hear the word *cancer*. The aftermath of it all is unexplainable. No one "gets it" unless they're by your side 24/7, like my mom is and always will be. But I have to say, I've not only learned life's greatest lessons, but I've also met unbelievable people throughout the journey. The friends I met during my illness actually know when I don't feel well, because they've dealt with it all themselves. We have a bond that will never be broken. I, personally, will never know the reason why I got brain cancer in the first place, but I can't change the past, all I can do is keep moving forward. Now that I'm looking at colleges, a different route has paved my career path. I am an aspiring student at Wheelock College in Boston, and want to study to become a child life specialist, myself. I won't ever give up.

Chapter 4

DREAMS DEFERRED

By Dana N. Laurie

On Thanksgiving in 2006, what were you doing? Eating turkey? Fighting over the last piece of cranberry sauce? Or maybe helping those less fortunate in a shelter?

I was in the hospital. 13 years old, being poked by needles and squeezed by electric blood pressure machines. This wasn't my first hospital visit, but it was my first inpatient visit.

"A pituitary tumor," the nurse told us the night before. My dad and I were sitting in the waiting room playing a Mario Cart game. I just started to cry.

The last time I remember crying that hard was when I read "Death Be Not Proud" by John J. Gunther. For those who have never read it, it was about the struggle of Johnny Gunther and his brain tumor. He died at age 17. (I am 16.)

For the next two and half years I was in MRI, CT-Scan, blood work, and doctor visit heaven. I even made a little song a couple weeks ago about it! It goes like this:

"48 blood tests, 18 MRIs, 9 great doctors, 6 ICU days, 5 CT scans, 3 hospitalizations, 2 surgeries, and a partridge in pear tree!"

If you stress the six ICU days when singing, it sounds better! Well the six Intensive Care Unit days should be explained to make more sense.

On June 17, 2009 (a bright sunny Wednesday), I went in for my Transsphenoidal (through the nose) Tumor Removal. After six hours, they took out 90% of the tumor. Claps for my neurosurgeon (Dr. Harter at NYU) and ENT specialist (Dr. Lebowitz at NYU). Boos for the constant headaches called insurance battles.

But every cloud that has a silver lining has a storm brewing on the inside. We went to my endocrinologist for my post-operation chat. He handed us the pathology report. And I was thrown the biggest curve ball of my live (thus far).

The tumor was not benign as we had thought. It was actually a teenage mutant ninja turtle! Just kidding, it was only mutant. So now, two months from the beginning of my junior year of high school, I am a cancer patient. No longer is it a pituitary adenoma, but a pituitary CARCINOMA. Hurrah.

Now that I have cancer, radiation is the next step. Sure, no problem. That starts this Monday, September 28, 2009.

But I should inform you of the other parts of my life.

I started my own eco-friendly, chemical free, color cosmetic company called Purus Cosmetics, thanks to the support of NFTE NY Metro and Prep for Prep. Without either of them I could not be where I am today.

I am from a program called Prep for Prep, which helps New York City public school students get into private day or boarding schools. They also have a great support system to help us get through anything.

But aside from that, I have my family.

Divorced parents, half-brother I just met (who rocks) and some crazy problems as you might imagine happening. I usually do not talk about it, but sometimes I want to scream in someone's head so they realize how much they are negatively affecting my life.

But I am the type of person who does not want to make other people unhappy or disappointed. However, with my two surgeries and this whole cancer experience, I now express my opinion and quirkiness where ever I go.

The reason is: You and I never know when we are going to leave this life. So what is the point of having secrets, being deceitful and encouraging drama?

With all of that under my belt, and always trying to be positive, I hope you can be grateful for everything in your life and live life to its fullest.

Don't defer your dreams, no matter what happens.

Chapter 5

A SUBURBAN LIFE

By Andrea Baatz

Bohemia. Many may research and unearth the title as a kingdom from long ago, placed in Europe, and filled with gorgeous mountains. For me, when I hear the term roll off a tongue, I associate it with my present-day home. Bohemia is a small town centrally located on Long Island, New York. It harbors mountains of automobiles and classic American families. It is made of many cul-de-sacs with identical housing neatly aligned, fenced in, and isolated. It is the faultless balance of properness and roughness, applicable to any aspect of life, like dialect, crime, education, friendship, and so on. An outsider might see our civilization as easy, simplistic, and maybe even boring; however, this promotes me to remember specifically the memories that deal with overcoming this, finding excitement, and originality, or the memories that do not fit this Bohemian pattern at all.

There were blizzard conditions on December 27, 1993, but this was the day of my birth. I was born into a family that consists of my father, mother, my sister and me, Andrea Marie Baatz. My family has always been the average middle-class household of individuals trying to make it through life together. For my parents this means juggling jobs, housework, and raising two children.

My mom has been in the nursing profession for countless years. Sometimes her career kept her away from us through late, forbidden hours. On these occasions, when my father said, "Come on, it's time for bed," I would blatantly use the excuse of, "I'm waiting for Mom," when in truth, I stayed up to watch the late night cartoons.

As years have gone by, it is hard not to think of how my mom's career affected my sister's and my upbringing. On one hand, it enabled her to shelter us and pamper us, but otherwise, my mom was not home extensively, which left my dad with the challenges of raising us. If we did not like food, we would spit it out, hide it under our plates, or give it to the dog. We made him learn to braid hair and re-learn elementary math. Within our shallow walls of suburban perfection, we had food fights, burping contests, crayon-colored walls, and booger covered playpens.

As my sister and I became older, my dad focused more on his self-employed careers. The new alone time together allowed my sister and me to develop both our relationship together and our individuality. Frequently, I was questioned how we ever got along; we were born polar-opposites. My sister is quite the athletic, extroverted type. I, on the other hand, am the nerdy, introverted kid. Still, growing up, we were the dynamic duo. She used to lug me around in our Barbie car, yet she stuck up for me on the school bus. We danced, rode horses, played video games, and compared muscles. This is when the trouble started, though, as life became more complex than either of us could have ever imagined.

When I was born, I was born with Multiple Hereditary Exostoses (MHE). MHE is a disease that causes the extra growth of bones. Having the disease doomed me to severe babysitting with X-rays and doctor's visits every six months to a year. This meant leaving school for hour drives, in order to see the tickle doctor.

One casual muscle comparison had led to great worry with my parents, and I remember being aggravated. I always thought my dad took all of my condition excessively seriously. I did not want to have to go back to the doctors, but we did.

One unforgettable moment of my life was waiting for my parents to come back after leaving me in this new doctor's exam room. For the first time, I had witnessed my father's wet eyes and reddened face.

My family already understood that my condition made me individualistic. One in 50,000 people are born with the situation; however, in my circumstance it was even furthermore unique when the osteochondroma, benign bone tumor, in my right humerus became a chondrosarcoma, a cancer of the cartilage. This is what my parents had learned, with the additional fact that I became the youngest person ever recorded with this condition at nine years old.

The drive home was confusing. My mom tried to explain what was going on. She began with, "You know those extra bone bumps that you have?"

"Yes," I replied.

"Well the one in your arm is a bad guy, and he's eating all your good bones now." Not even until recently do I think I have understood the severity of the situation.

The new discovery led to a series of tests: an MRI, bone scans, cat scans, X-rays, physicals, blood tests, and a biopsy. The bone scan was a different experience. It required a shot to make my insides illuminate. Certainly, I was crying, which made the resident nervous, and so after putting the blue elastic rubber band around my arm, he left for a long period. I tugged and tested the flexibility of it waiting impatiently. My arm was changing colors and becoming itchy. I was gaining anxiety and my parents were simply furious. It turned out he went to retrieve an actual doctor to do the procedure.

I had the biopsy done at Schneider's Children Hospital. The place appeared incredible at first, but after waiting in the lobby, we were relocated to the waiting room, which could only hold the feeling of tension. I met with the anesthesiologist, who saw my weary face and told me all about her Husky dog. I got into my hospital gown and walked into the room. It was sterile white. I went to sleep and afterwards I had two stitches. I hoped never to see that room again. Unfortunately, it was revealed, I would indeed return, the next time for surgery.

The night before, my aunt met me at my horseback riding lesson and gave me a big black stuffed lab.

That rests as one of the last times I ever got on a horse again.

The next day, we went to the same waiting room. The anesthesiologist was there as well, and she showed me a picture of her dog. I returned to the detrimental white room, my stuffed rabbit, named Fuzzy, in hand, and hospital gown on. I received a shot and a mask smothered me. There was counting and I was asleep.

Upon waking, I was most upset that my aunt did not say goodbye to me, although she had and I just did not remember. My mom surprised me with Fuzzy. He had on a bathrobe and a sling on his right arm just like me. This initiated my stay at the hospital.

The first room I shared with a roommate who had an upside down stomach. I was embarrassed for my family member who could not bear to stay and visit due to the smell of vomit lingering from the little girl lying in the next bed over. I was so astounded to experience the feelings that I felt for that young girl. Always sheltered, I never would have thought that things like that existed, and to this day, I wonder how she is.

In my second room, I was by the window. One day my mom asked my roommate if she would like her blinds opened, but the act was refused because she was allergic to the sun. I was shocked at the disability this girl had, but she became my new friend. Her name was Ariel. We played cards together. She taught me how to play Kings in the Corner.

There was a terrible doctor there who would wake me in the early hours and shred my bandage off. I loathed him. The first time I saw my scar I became a wreck. I was disgusted at the sight of my staples, and I stopped eating for a week, until the best night of my stay, when my mother made a Thanksgiving dinner. My family was there and so was Ariel's, and we all dined together. It felt like suburban living once again.

On one of the last days there, I went with my mom to do arts and crafts. I made a doll there, but more important, I experienced deep jealousy of this young girl. She had had a brain tumor, and she had to wear a plastic protector of her IVs. For this reason, my mother had to help her make the doll because the protector restricted the girl from constructing it herself. I was her daughter; she needed to be helping me. I felt guilty afterwards.

While there, I also made Ariel a colorful leaf from tissue paper. Before I left, my mom hung up the leaf on Ariel's corkboard. She was not there for me to say goodbye.

The day we left, I visited the Ronald McDonald house, which is where my family stayed. I often wonder how the experience affected my family. How had they perceived the situation?

Upon returning home, I was home schooled. When the tutor came, she often scolded me for not completing my work, although I was always an "A" student. I remember feeling obstinate because "the strange lady most definitely did not understand me and my circumstances." I had physical therapy from a man with weird salt and pepper hair that called me a "skooch." I was not fond of these meetings.

Although I visited class on picture day, reintegrating into school completely was a challenge. So many people wanted to know what was wrong, and suddenly wanted to be my friend.

The experience took a great toll on my outlook of life. I began seeing and thinking more maturely. In addition, it was difficult for a young child like me to understand the circumstances and severity of the whole thing. However, these complications helped me to morph into the person I am today.

Today, I am sure that hardly any days go by without me being reminded of my past. During my daily activities, people often see my scar and make remarks about it. I tell them a watered down story refraining from any use of the word *cancer*, worrying about others' judgment. Quite often the responses I receive show I have misguided them as they remark things such as, "You should tell people you were bitten by a shark." It bothers me that in society a person's survival story has to be entertaining in order to be thought deeply about, when in fact just each ordinary day a person lives is a miracle worth a moment of sentimentality.

For people who do know the truth of my story, however, they too often remind me of it. Since the day I returned home from the hospital, I have been told some things that I will never be able to do, being too strenuous for my arm. When told this, I am inclined to think how my life would have changed without the surgery. For one thing, I might have been an athlete, but for another, I might not have been an artist. Having the surgery meant limited amount of physical activity and no participation in elementary school gym class. So instead, I went to art classes. I believe that this time truly started my interest in this creative outlet that has lasted through to my age now.

I may have hated the idea of physical therapy, a loss of independence, the painful bandage changes, and the questions and fake friendships. However, until now, I have never so much appreciated the experience and the effect it has had on my life. It is strange, but sometimes I feel closer to the people I met in the hospital than to my current friends I have. While I have not seen those roommates and nurses for roughly eight years, I know that they have an understanding of life that we can share.

Overall, by embracing the fear a hospital bestows upon any patient and encompassing the feeling of love, which my friends, family, and doctors expressed, I have realized that no family suburban life could ever be typical. Our houses may look the same, and our cars may run through the same process, but you will realize that in no way is anyone perfect or exactly alike in comparison to another. If you have not realized all of the surprises life has in store, such as this, perhaps it is time to open that freshly painted white picket fence, and explore the world you just do not understand yet. Understand the impediments that all people are comprised of and have learned to live with. Understand the deeper meaning in your surroundings and make sense of humanity. Understand how you can make a difference.

Chapter 6

THE BROCCOLI RABE BLOG STORY

By Donna Coane

In August 2010 I must have been told by my pediatrician a million times that whatever I had was a sinus infection, but I never believed it. My face was swelling up, half of my face felt numb and my nose was constantly dripping. I went to an ENT doctor in September and after one look at me, he ordered a CT scan immediately.

The next day as I walked through the school, I was looking forward to staying after for club meetings. A few minutes before school ended, the principal came into my classroom and told me that my mom was at the school to pick me up. I argued with her that I had to stay after school for club meeting, but she told me I had to go to the city hospital right away. I wouldn't learn until weeks later that my mom had spent that whole day crying in the doctor's office after seeing the results of the CT scan. The CT scan showed that there was a huge tumor in my face.

I remember sitting in the hospital not knowing what was going on, no one wanted to tell me anything till they were absolutely sure I had cancer. The doctors finally did a biopsy of the tumor and after a couple of weeks they told me that it was cancerous. It wasn't till the end of September 2010 that I was diagnosed with the rare tissue cancer called Alveolar Rhabdomyosarcoma in my sinus cavity, my jaw, around my eye and in the lining of my brain. The doctors spoke of surgically removing the tumor and rebuilding my face, but one doctor wanted to start chemotherapy first to see if the tumor would shrink. After one chemotherapy treatment the swelling in my face went down; the doctors decided to just use chemotherapy and radiation to treat me.

Going to the hospital in the city was very hard for me. I hated being so far away from my home in Long Island. After a couple months of treatment, I asked if I could be switched over to Stony Brook University hospital, which was only a half hour from my house. My doctor was very hesitant about switching me over until I ended up in Stony Brook's ER. One night after treatment, my fever shot up to 104 degrees, which could be lethal to a cancer patient. My mom rushed me over to Stony Brook's ER at 3 am so I could receive antibiotics. The nurses and doctors at Stony Brook were so nice I begged my doctor to switch me over to the university's hospital. Before Christmas of 2010 I was finally being treated at Stony Brook's children's hospital and pediatric cancer center.

Receiving treatment at Stony Brook was very different than the city hospital. There was a huge room full of toys and crafts for the pediatric patients to play in and meet one another. The nurses were much friendlier and became my friends during treatment. There was a parent room with dining tables and chairs for visitors to sit down and relax. Sometimes I would ask my mom to bring me food from home and I would eat in there to get out of my room. The rooms were brighter with big widows for sunlight to come through. You could see all of Long Island from the windows. Being closer to home meant that my friends and family could visit me in the hospital, too, which helped me emotionally. I realized then that when I felt happy chemotherapy treatments went by faster.

Even though things were looking good and chemotherapy treatments were working, there was always a bump in the road. My new doctor at Stony Brook decided to do radiation treatments and chemotherapy treatments at the same time to attack the cancer. I did a full month of radiation treatments and then started to develop mouth sores. There were only three more radiation treatments left when I had to be hospitalized because the mouth sores got so bad that I couldn't eat, drink or talk. The sores were in my gums, on my tongue, and down my throat. I had to resort to writing down what I wanted to say for weeks before I could talk. I spent three months in the hospital getting intravenous nutrition, antibiotics, and pain medicine. The hospital wouldn't let me leave till I could start to eat on my own again. During this hospitalization my mom had to drive through some of the worst blizzards Long Island had ever experienced just to visit me. My mouth sores caused me so much pain when I tried to eat that I lost a lot of weight; I was given special weight gaining shakes in order to get back to healthy weight. Even though I survived this horrible occurrence of mouth sores, I would get them every couple of months during my year and a half of cancer treatment, but now that I knew how to heal mouth sores from my first time having them, the mouth sores I had later in my treatments weren't that bad.

I met a lot of other cancer patients at Stony Brook, one of them being a four-year-old girl named Darianna. I was put in a hospital room at the time that had Tinker Bell decals on the walls. She had seen the decals and I heard her outside of my door. I invited her into my room with her mom and introduced myself to her. After she left to go back to her room, my nurse told me that Darianna had just been diagnosed with terminal brain cancer. I wanted to cheer Darianna up so badly that in the middle of the night I drew a bunch of pictures of Tinker Bell and told my nurse to give them to Darianna. We were both in and out of the hospital for our chemotherapy treatment, but we always hung out together when we were both there at the same time. I would learn a few months after I finished my cancer treatment that she had passed away from her cancer at the age of five.

There was another cancer patient I became very close friends with, but he wasn't being treated at Stony Brook like me. He was my classmate Joey; we had been in a couple of the same classes and had a lot of friends in common. Joey and I were diagnosed with cancer around the same time, which shocked the high school. Joey had been diagnosed with cancer at Stony Brook, but chose to get treated at Sloan Hospital in the city. We kept in contact through Facebook and texting and became close friends even though we never saw each other during our cancer treatments. We always spoke of coming back to school as cancer survivors and what colleges we were planning to go to. Unfortunately, a month after I had returned to school as a cancer survivor, Joey died from a stroke. All of my classmates grieved for weeks; I grieved for months.

Having cancer taught me something very important: to be happy and make others happy. I feel that because I reminded myself to be happy during my cancer that I survived. I lost two of my good friends during to cancer and I wanted to help others who have cancer. During my cancer journey I made a video journal on YouTube to help other pediatric cancer patients (www.youtube.com/user/BroccoliRabeBlog). I named it BroccoliRabeBlog because my cancer Rhabdomyosarcoma sounded like my favorite side dish Broccoli Rabe. After I had finished my cancer treatment in January 2012, I heard that the American Cancer Society was holding an event at my high school called Relay For Life, I signed up for it right away and made a relay team to join me. I raised over $4,000 for American Cancer Society with the help of family and friends. During the event I was asked to do a speech during opening ceremonies. I told everyone there about how important I found it was to be happy and make others happy. Even though I'm done with chemotherapy and radiation, I still experience side effects from the treatments like neuropathy pain, but I always remember to stay happy and make others happy.

Chapter 7

CANCER... CANCER

By Samantha Ashburn

I thought only adults could get this, I never thought I would. May 24, 2007, waiting in a little dark room at Kaiser not knowing what was happening nor what was going to happen, sitting in a wheelchair holding my mom's hand, waiting for the doctor to come in and just say I had a broken leg—not wanting to hear the words the doctor was about to say: Samantha, the pain in your leg is being caused by a tumor. Those words were like a knife stabbing through my body. The tears just seemed to fall like rain. He said it could be cancer or just a regular tumor, but the only way to find out was to do a needle biopsy that night. As they got me ready for the biopsy, all I thought of was the tumor. I didn't know what cancer was, so I didn't worry about that. While lying on the bed and trying to relax and stay calm, I couldn't stop my tears. They stuck a needle that seemed like 2 feet long in my right knee with a camera on the end of it. I was watching them the whole time, seeing the blood drip everywhere, them moving the camera in my knee around, them taking parts of the tumor out. About an hour later we were able to go home, and the results would be back in about 7 days.

Home didn't seem the same after being told I had a tumor. My house seemed to always have people over, and everyone was always trying to make me smile. We didn't let too many people know what was going on only 'cause I wasn't comfortable with people knowing I had a tumor. Days went by not knowing what was wrong. The fear in my mom's face got worse each minute of the day. The phone call we were all waiting for turned out to be a call that we didn't want to hear. The doctor told my mom that the results of the needle biopsy came back inconclusive and that we needed to have another biopsy, which would mean surgery in Oakland with the tumor remover surgeon.

June 7, 2007, 6:00 a.m. arriving in Oakland's Kaiser 2nd floor. My best friend Margaret had come with my mom and stepdad. As they were getting the operating room ready, they were giving me all kinds of meds to take that were making me super goofy and tired. I was in an ugly gown with a weird hat on my head. As they were ready to push me out of the room my mom was in, I started to freak. I was screaming and screaming for my mom, and they wouldn't let her come with me. They had me on the bed and told me they were putting some laughing gas in me, and I would feel all happy and calm. They told me to count back from 10. I only remember getting to 8.

Waking up in the recovery room, I was confused, sick, drugged, and just very upset. I couldn't stop crying or puking. I was so miserable, I have never felt that way. I was in recovery for about 3 hours. They weren't sure if they were going to let me go home since I wasn't coming out of all the drugs the way I should have. Finally, I was sent home, lying in the back seat drugged up on painkillers, out of my mind. We got home around 7, and my stepdad laid me on the couch. I was finally waking up and becoming more talkative and, of course, the house was full of people, all making sure I was ok. This time we had to wait about 6-7 days for the results.

June 12, 2007, the day my life changed. My mom was told I had osteosarcoma in the right femur/knee. She couldn't believe it—her 12 year old daughter with cancer. That evening my mom came home and the look on her face wasn't too good. She said, "Baby girl, you know I love you, but the doctor called and said that the results came back and you do have cancer." Those words killed me. I just sat there letting the tears run from my face. I still didn't know what cancer was, but I knew it wasn't good. I stayed in my room all the time. I didn't want anyone knowing I was sick. The days seemed to go by so slow, and I just couldn't get over the fact I, Samantha Ashburn, had cancer.

June 14, 2007, I meet with my new-to-be family, A.K.A. my oncology doctors. I had 3 of them. My family and I met with the head oncology doctor, and I did not like him. He went over the chemo I would be on, the things to expect, what would happen to me, my survival rate to the kind of cancer I had (which was only 80 percent chance I would make it), and so many other things. He then told me that I was going to lose my hair!! I had long brown beautiful hair, and there was no way I was going to lose it. I told him I would rather die than be bald. When I said that, the look on everyone's face was shocked. That's when Dr. Kieghly got on my bad side. Before I could start chemo, I needed to do all these tests and get a brovica put in my chest in order to start chemo.

After hearing all of what the doctors had to say to my family, I just wanted to wake up one day and wish it was a nightmare. All I could think of was: Why Me? What did I do to deserve this? Was it because I talked back to my mom? Didn't listen? That's one question my doctors or family could not an-swer. I started doing my own research and talking to other kids with my type of cancer. I then got some faith that everything was going to be all right, and I could make it through this battle. A week before I started chemo, my older brother told me he would shave his head with me, which was a shocker (he loves his hair). So my mom took us to get our hair cut. He shaved his first, then next was me. When the lady cut my ponytail off, I broke down in tears. I could not shave it, so I got it super short, and after that I got to dye it hot pink.

June 19, 2007, first round of chemo. I was sore after getting my brovica put in that morning, tired and scared of not knowing what was going to happen, not knowing if I was really going to get sick. I remember the first 5 minutes of chemo I was feeling good, not sick or anything. About right after I told that to my mom, it changed. I was crying, screaming, puking, and just felt like crap. Words can't explain how bad it was. The sickness lasted for 3 days, the worst days in my life.

Each chemo round had its ups and downs. Some were fine, some were just awful. I learned what medications worked the best or just made me forget about everything. After about 4 rounds and not eating, I started losing weight dramatically. I went from 110 pounds to only 82.5 pounds in only 4 weeks. I had to get 16 feeding tubes, but that didn't stop me from losing the weight. I kept losing weight day after day. I would just lay in my room looking at the ceiling, depressed and lonely even though I had my family, friends, and community. I still felt like I was in a cave with no one there. No one knew how I felt or what I was going though. They didn't understand my pain.

About two months into chemo, I started meeting some cancer kids that I knew would understand me and my pain. I met Ben who was a boy who had cancer in his eyes and they were removed at age 2, but he never let that stop him from doing things. Ben could always make you smile and laugh. He was so funny, and his faith in God was so amazing. Then I met Jesse, who had a similar cancer as me, and boy was he so funny and would talk for hours and hours about things. He was like my brother. Next I met my big sister Becky. We shared so much besides the same cancer we had. I could go to her for anything, and we told each other so much. Then I got to meet Austin, this funny, laid back, nice caring person. We hit it off so well. We always would hang out in the hospital and tell jokes, too. I also got close with the nurses, my 2nd family.

A few months went by. We did the same thing: chemo, home, hospital. I was then bald and not too happy about it, but I was getting over the "I HATE MY LIFE" stage and accepting the fact that I had cancer. The best part of having cancer were the friends I made, the things I got to do like be on TV, play the cancer card—you could say I used cancer to the fullest. I always tried to make sure I never let cancer bring me down. I figured that if I have to deal with this, then I'm going to use it the max, and I sure did. I became close with all my nurses and staff. I had my favorite nurses, and I had some mean ones. Finally, I was down to only 10 rounds of chemo, and the countdown was on. When I made it to round 3, I had a stroke from all the chemo, which made me go to ICU for about 2 weeks. Then I got to go back to the ward, which was my family. I felt too out of place in ICU, and the people there were just not that kind. I had to end chemo early because it started to hurt me rather than help me.

February 14, 2008, CANCER FREE on Valentine's Day, the best day in my life. But it was also a sad day. Strange thing to say but true. Hearing that I was cancer free and wasn't going to receive any chemo made me cry. For a year that's all I've known: get chemo, hospital, needles, pain, sickness, crying, fevers, rashes, and much more. Then to just stop, it was hard. I became close to my nurses and all the staff at Kaiser. It hurt leaving them, but I knew it was for the best.

My life started to get back to normal, I started school, my hair was growing back, and I was meeting new friends. Everything seemed to be prefect until I got the news that my best friend Ben was dying of cancer, and there was nothing else they could do for him. I got to see him 2 days before he passed away, and I think that was the hardest thing in my life, giving him one last hug and seeing him look so weak and sick. He passed away on January 19, 2009. Then on January 20, 2009, I received the news that my "big sister" passed away from cancer. Becky wasn't really my sister, but we became so close and shared so many things. I wasn't able to say goodbye to her, but I knew she was sick. She told me she was dying, but half of me didn't want to believe it. I was severely depressed about losing them. I just wanted to give up on life and I pretty much did. Then 3 months later I got the news, my other friend Jesse passed away, and on my 14 th birthday I went to his funeral. After losing my friends, it was like my heart was just torn and gone. I only had one friend left that I met who had cancer, and the thought of losing him was hard, but I'm happy to say he's doing really well.

Cancer came with many struggles. Some seemed impossible to overcome, but I did. I couldn't have done it without my family and friends. Even though my 3 closest friends aren't here on Earth, they're still with me in my heart and they're my motivation. I can honestly say having cancer has changed me and my life in many ways, and I know what it means to fight and live life!

Chapter 8

LIFE IS A JOURNEY, NOT A DESTINATION

By Saul Tbeile

My name is Saul Tbeile. I am one of the many people that have ventured on a journey. Thankfully, I am also one of the many to complete this journey, which all too many people have not been able to complete.

It started off like any other day, when I was about to turn 12. My mom, ever so observant, noticed that I had had black and blue marks for about two months that seemed to keep getting worse. Because of this, combined with a constant nosebleed, a rash called petechiae, and that I had been falling asleep the second I came home from school, when I usually stayed up till at least 10, she knew something was wrong. The next day, when I complained of a huge headache, my mom decided that this was the perfect time to take me to the doctor. Unknowingly, I embarked on a journey that would change my life.

When I first got to the doctor I thought, "Nice. I might miss a couple of days of school." If only I knew how true that statement that would be. The doctor told me to go get a blood test. It was then that I started to get a little suspicious that something might be up.

That night my mom got a call from the doctor saying that he wanted me to go to the ER immediately. Later on, my dad would say that he realized then that I had leukemia, and his mind just hadn't connected the dots because you never expect it to happen to someone you know. Thankfully, my mom told the doctor that I was sleeping and she would bring me first thing in the morning. Little did I know that it would be the last time I would sleep in my bed for about two weeks.

The next morning, at about 6:30, my parents woke me up and rushed me to the ER. On the way, I vividly remember the scene in the car. We were driving up an incline near Maimonides Hospital and I asked my parents these exact words, "Hey, mom, I never thought I would say this, but can I go to school today?"

We got to the waiting room and waited about an hour until we finally got called in. I remember the fight that the doctors had to get me to put in the IV. Maybe subconsciously I was fighting the inevitable. Maybe my unconscious did not want to acknowledge the situation; I don't really know. After the doctors finally got the IV in and did the blood test, we waited for the results. Sadly, I tested positive for leukemia; to be specific, "acute lymphoblastic leukemia," or ALL, for short. In about five seconds, my whole world was shattered. How can I possibly have cancer? I was healthy; I was just an ordinary kid.

My mom and dad were hysterical. I was their oldest son, and I was just diagnosed with cancer. Me, well, I was in shock.

After the immediate shock wore off, I had a lot of questions. As an Orthodox Jew, what would I do for food since I can only eat kosher? Will the hospital have kosher food? What about school? Will I be able to go back this year? How would I keep up with all the work? What will happen with all my friends? Will I ever have a normal life again? And the biggest question of all: Will I even survive? My brain was working in overdrive trying to answer all these questions.

They took me up to the Intensive Care Unit. Thinking back, I think the ICU may be the one of the worst parts of the experience. Since it was an ICU, they needed to keep me under observation, so I had no privacy and worse, no bathroom. The next day, my mother was contacted by a cancer organization called Chai Lifeline, and started to work on getting me transferred to a hospital that specializes in cancer. The night before I was scheduled to start on chemotherapy, Chai Lifeline called an ambulance to transfer me to Memorial Sloan Kettering Cancer Center. That night I started chemo. I honestly don't really remember the next two weeks. The only thing I remember was asking the doctors to try to get me out by my birthday, February 24th. And that was exactly what they did; I got out of the hospital on the 21st of February.

After that, my life more or less fell into a routine. Every day I would wake up, drive to Manhattan, get hooked up with the poison or poisons of the day, wait between eight and ten hours watching *Everyone Loves Raymond* or reading a book, and then go home and pass out. That was basically my life for the first two to three months of treatment.

During this time, I received visits from my friends and family almost every day. Behind the scenes, Chai Lifeline, my school, and my mother were trying to work out some way for me to "go to school" while not actually being in class. Together they came up with an idea: to have me learn through Skype. The teacher would set it up in the room, and I would be a part of the class. Sadly, this was earlier on, about three years ago, when this sort of thing wasn't as reliable as it is today. In fact, today many colleges offer courses online through a program similar to this. It didn't work out in the end, and some teachers ended up coming by to home-school me.

Throughout this time, and for the rest of my treatment, two volunteers continuously visited me, and that helped me immensely—whether it was physically helping me or mentally helping me feel like a normal person, not some fragile invalid that needed to be locked up. Later on in my treatment, I met another volunteer who literally became a brother to me in everything except blood. Every day, I spoke to him for hours upon hours until he got married and moved out of the country.

Midway through treatment, I was finally able to go out into the world—when my neutrophil count was good, that is. It was then that I fully appreciated every day and tried to enjoy it to its fullest. I started to pursue cooking. It was like therapy for me; some people read, some people play an instrument, cooking was my medium. So every day I would cook something new: one day lo mein, the next pull-apart pizza. Every day something new. In the morning, I would wake up, make brunch with my mother, put on Food Network, decide on something to make for lunch, read an entire book, make dinner with my mom, and then read some more. There is something about cooking the food yourself that just makes it taste so much better. Cooking for me can be likened to a mini-game; while not the main focus of the game, it makes it more enjoyable. That was exactly what it did. While I was still undergoing chemo and couldn't leave the house, it made my life much more enjoyable.

I also started to read a tremendous amount. I have always been a good reader, but with all the time I had on my hands, I was able to read even more. I devoured books like they were water. I own every Clive Cussler book and most of Tom Clancy's novels, among many others. Each book is its own little adventure, and just like the main characters succeeded in the end, so did I.

Throughout all this I learned many important lessons, specifically from three volunteers, two of whom I still speak with almost every day, even now after I have finished treatment. One important lesson is that every day is a new adventure. Recently, a close friend of mine passed away from cancer. He always believed that everyday brought another adventure. That is how I remember him.

I have learned that every day there is something new to discover. Whether in school, and it is something interesting in biology, or outside of school, and we are visiting the elderly in a hospital, there is always something new to experience and discover. But along with new adventures, every day also brings new challenges. These challenges help mold you into a better person in the long run, even if it doesn't seem like that in the short term.

To me, those last few lines sum up my journey through cancer: another challenge to overcome, in the even greater adventure called life. Even though it was a grueling experience and I wouldn't wish it upon my worst enemy, it also helped mold me into the person I am today, proving true what Ralph Waldo Emerson said, "Life is a journey, not a destination."

Chapter 9

ME AND MY LEUKEMIA

By Mallory Evans

Two years have passed, so much has happened. From slipping in science class, to losing my hair and taking thirty pills a day. With having multiple blood and platelet transfusions just to keep you going and mini-strokes happening because of the poisons healing my body. Having leukemia, you learn you have to get sicker before you can get better.

On a warm week day in August, I slipped in the sixth grade science classroom. Right away a huge bruise appeared and that night I started running fever. I went to the doctor's office and the diagnosis was a sinus infection. So they sent us home with antibiotics and told us it would clear right up. After a couple of weeks the fever and bruise were still there and had not at all faded.

My grandfather, who is a doctor, told my mother to get blood work for me. At the doctor's office, the nurse was trying to get my veins, but they kept collapsing. I had to get poked at least twelve times over the course of one to two days before they sent us to the children's satellite hospital in Parker. Only there did the person finally get my vein and draw blood. When the doctor called with the results, he told us not to come back, but to go to The

Children's Hospital in Denver and that they had already made an appointment at the hematology and oncology clinic there.

When we arrived there, we checked in and waited for someone to take us back. While we waited I became more and more anxious. About thirty minutes later someone finally came and got us. First they took my vitals, then they drew more blood, and third they took us to a room to wait for the results and the doctor. The doctor eventually showed up with a new diagnosis, the blood work had come back showing blasts, meaning leukemia, which is a type of cancer. Right then my entire life changed, I thought my life would be over at age eleven.

I had to stay at the hospital for about a week. Over the course of that week, I had found out that my cancer was Acute Lymphocytic Leukemia (ALL) pre-B cell. Within 24 hours of finding out, I had my medi-port surgically placed. Also by the end of the week, I had received my first chemo. During my first bone marrow aspiration and spinal tap, I also received my first blood transfusion.

When we got home the first thing we did was cut my hair to shoulder length. (I still have my ponytail of hair, I couldn't donate it because I had already had my first chemo.) I was diagnosed September 13, 2006 and had very little hair by the beginning of November, and by that time I decided to have my sister Katie shave my head. It is very hard to go from having hair down to your waist to having to wear a hat just because there is not a single strand of hair to keep you warm.

With cancer, or leukemia to be more specific, comes IV chemo and lots of pills. Before having cancer I had never taken a pill; after becoming sick I had to take at least thirty pills a day, and at least once a week I had to get treatment at the hospital. If I was lucky, I would make it through the week without having a blood or platelet transfusion. One time we waited too long for a blood transfusion. I could hardly lift myself off my bed.

When you are low on red blood cells, there's not enough oxygen in your blood stream, so you get very tired and your heart will start pounding after just a little bit of movement. So this time, since we had waited so long, I blacked out for just a second, but almost passed out from being so low. The great thing is, after you receive the transfusion, you immediately feel much better. Platelet transfusions are a little different; you don't really know when you are low unless you start bleeding very easily. When I get a platelet transfusion I start feeling tightness in my chest and begin wheezing. My oncologist just figures that I'm allergic to them so I just keep my inhaler nearby and pre-med with Benadryl and Tylenol.

About nine months into treatment on Mother's Day 2007, I wasn't feeling so well, so I took a nap in the afternoon. By early evening I woke up, and when I went to eat dinner, I couldn't use my right hand to get the fork to my mouth.

Within a couple of hours I was completely paralyzed on the right side of my body, and we were on our way to the Emergency Room. During the ride over, it resolved and was okay, and I could move my arm and leg. At the ER they took blood work and examined me. Everything was ok. They couldn't figure out what was wrong because my symptoms had disappeared, except I was neutropenic (low blood counts, nothing to fight with) and low on platelets. We had our usual scheduled appointment at the oncology clinic the next morning, so by 2:30am we were on our way home only to return by 8:00am Monday.

After a few hours of sleep, we returned to the hospital. While getting ready for my platelet transfusion, my arm started feeling funny while getting my vitals taken, like it did the night before. The nurse brought us to my room where I would receive my platelets, and another nurse brings in Tylenol and hands them to me. But I can't bring my hand up high enough to grab them. This is when we know it is happening again.

The nurse injects Benadryl in to the pump that infuses medicines into my medi-port. So immediately I fall asleep and slept during my whole transfusion. When I wake up next, it's to my oncologist's voice, and at this point my entire right side is numb. I was trying to say something but was slurring my words. As soon as she looked at me, she said, "Her lip is drooping, we need a cat scan NOW!"

So she got me a wheelchair as she was calling out orders to the charge nurse to call downstairs, "And tell them I AM bringing her myself!" Off to radiology we went. Normally a nurse will take you down, but not this time.

Doctor Kerry was taking me down personally. My mom was so scared and so was I!

I was completely paralyzed on the right side of my body and was having mini strokes. I was hospitalized for a week. Over that week I had an EEG, an MRI and 2 cat-scans. I had to have a separate line (IV) other than my mediport run, and it took 4 nurses and several hours and pokes to get to my vein! Finally we had to leave the inpatient floor, go down stairs and get an ER nurse and a paramedic to do it! After several days of presenting and resolving and lots and lots of tests, my doctors came to the conclusion that the chemo they injected into my cerebral fluid during a spinal tap had caused a toxic reaction. It usually happens with kids that are getting a higher dose chemo. I am just extremely sensitive to all the meds. I still had to take that kind of chemo, but I had to take a "rescue drug" 42 hours after my procedure to reverse the effects. Thankfully it never happened again!

Poison heals my body, nothing else. I will have completed 30 months of chemotherapy by the time I am finished with treatment. A lot has happened to me since I was diagnosed 3 years ago! I have definitely learned with cancer you have to get sicker before you can get better!

Chapter 10

CANCER KICKOFF

By Kalyn Faller

I remember the day my life changed as if it was yesterday. It was Super Bowl Sunday 2010, Saints vs. Colts. At the time I was a 14-year-old football fanatic. I looked forward to the Super Bowl as much as I looked forward to Christmas. But this year was different; I spent the entire day in bed with stomach pains. My mom knew something was really wrong when I did not even get up for kickoff. She could feel I had a fever, so she took my temperature. The expression on her face went from calm to concerned as soon as 102° appeared on the thermometer screen. My mom's first instinct was to take me to the hospital. Little did I know this would be the first of many trips to come.

The following 72 hours would later be known as the longest three days of my life. It consisted of me being poked and prodded more times than I could count.

Day one was detection day at the hospital. Nurses and doctors were in and out of my room running test after test to figure out what was wrong. Finally a nurse suggested that I get a CT scan of my abdomen. When the results came back, she said that they saw a tiny mass that should not be there. I proceeded to get my first sonogram, which confirmed that I had a cyst on my right ovary. When I returned to my room there were three doctors waiting for me. In very serious voices they told my mom and I that I needed surgery to remove this cyst, but that there was a 1% chance of it being a cancerous tumor. I could feel the color escape my face when I heard those two words, "cancerous tumor." My mom made the smart decision to deny surgery right then and there, and instead get a second opinion the following day.

Day two was inquiry day with a second opinion. Dr. Davidson was the nicest man I had ever met. He approached my case with such sensitivity because he knew I was scared. He understood that I was a teenager with a mind-set of invincibility. But he too had bad news to deliver, sadly that news was for me. His assistant brought us into his very cozy office filled with impressive plaques and diplomas. When Dr. Davidson entered, I knew something was wrong by the look on his face. He sat down behind his giant desk and explained that the doctors at the hospital were correct. I did have a cyst on my right ovary that needed to be removed. And then in his serious voice he proceeded to add that the chances of it being a cancerous tumor were actually 50% not 1%. And there were those two words again that weighed on me like a boulder, "cancerous tumor." While I sat there trying to fight off the tears that wanted to come out, Dr. Davidson explained how he would not be performing the surgery. Instead he referred us to an oncologist that we could see the following day. I'll never forget Dr. Davidson.

Day three was comprehension day with the oncologist. When I arrived at Dr. White's office, I had this unusual positive attitude that I did not have in the last few days. I knew I needed to take care of whatever was going on, and that Dr. White was the only one that could make that possible. After getting examined and having blood tests done, it was time to talk to Dr. White. Instead of an assistant coming to get us and bring us to an office, Dr. White herself came and brought us to this big open room with comfy chairs and no desk. I found it strange how she sat next to me instead of my mom. Unlike other doctors I had met, she did not read off of my files. She put her chart down and looked me straight in the eye. She explained to me how it was not a cyst on my right ovary, but rather a tumor. In order to find out whether this tumor was cancerous or not she would have to perform a complicated surgery.

I immediately asked what percent there was of it being cancerous. She replied simply in a calm voice that there was a 75% chance of it being a cancerous tumor. Those two words "cancerous tumor" didn't affect me at all this time. I was ready to fight this head on and not let fear overcome me.

For the 4 months that followed that appointment, my life was put in survival mode. It began with the surgery that not only removed the tumor, but also removed my right ovary and fallopian tube. After a six-week recovery filled with pain and suffering, it was time to face my fears. Was the tumor cancerous or not? Dr. White sat us down in the big open room with comfy chairs again, but this time she sat next to my mom. She picked up her chart and proceeded to read off the procedure she performed six weeks prior. The last thing I remember hearing her say before I zoned out was "I removed a malignant cancerous tumor the size of a football from you." I could feel the room immediately shrink around me. My stomach was twisting and turning so much that the only thing I could do was stand up and face the wall. So many things were going through my mind at once, I did not know how to process anything. When I finally gained the courage to turn around and face Dr. White, I had tears streaming down my face. The only words I could manage to say were, "Will I be able to graduate junior high school?" To this day, I am still not sure why I chose to worry about school first of all things, but I am glad I did. In Dr. White's original plan for my chemotherapy schedule, I would not have been able to graduate on time with my classmates. After begging and pleading to begin treatment as soon as possible, she finally agreed. Even though I ended up getting my way and graduating on time, I will always remember this day as the worst day of my life.

The memories from my three months of chemotherapy have all combined into one giant nightmare. A nightmare that consisted of numerous needles, scans, blood tests, and trips to the hospital. In a matter of three months I spent over 35 days in Sloan Kettering Memorial Hospital. The worst part about chemotherapy was not the treatment itself or being imprisoned within the hospital, but the aftermath of it all. By aftermath I mean the hair loss, the hearing impairments, and the energy loss. Losing my hair made it evident to the world that I was sick, and in a way, helpless. My temporary hearing impairments prevented me from leaving the house most days because even the sound of car brakes would make me cringe. And the energy loss that still affects me today has prevented me from living each day to its fullest potential. But every poke and every prod was worth it on May 15, 2010. This was the official day of my remission.

In the last three years of being cancer free, I have learned to let go of the anger I once had about my original diagnosis. Instead I have embraced all the knowledge my disease has given me. I now know as a 17-year-old that life is too short to waste it on something that does not make you happy. And what makes me happy is helping others. I have volunteered and shared my story with so many incredible people over the last three years. Most recently I participated on a five-day service trip to Camden, New Jersey. It was there where I met with 11 amazing individuals that inspired me to share my story with Gilda's Club of New York City.

Being a cancer patient has given me the opportunity to be inspired, and also to inspire others to fight and chase their own dreams. I would not change a thing about my cancer journey because it made me who I am today, a survivor.

PART 2

MY PARENTS

Chapter 11

A SOFT BLOW

By Kayla Halvey

I was riding the train into my neighborhood with my boyfriend Danny when I found out the news. I had known it was a tumor for about a week at the time, but we were unsure as to whether it was benign or malignant. The words have been haunting me all week. *Benign or malignant—he won't eat, he's losing weight. Benign or malignant - he won't go out, he just stays in bed waiting for the pain to stop. Benign or malignant—the doctors can't find anything. Benign or malignant—his colon his fine though. Benign or malignant—it might just be a bacterial infection. Benign or malignant—a tumor between his stomach and pancreas. Benign or malignant—not the pancreas, oh God, anything but the pancreas. Benign or mal—*

"Kayla, it's pancreatic. Daddy is going to start treatment in a few weeks," she says over the phone. Danny and I wait for a shuttle train to take us back to Rockaway Park. I hug Danny and loudly whisper, "I fucking hate doctors. Ignorant bastards." I'm not crying, but tears drip down on his shoulders as I rant to him about how long my dad has had the symptoms, and how it took a year and half and three doctors to find something as distinct as a goddamn *tumor* lodged in his pancreas. He knows that it's a death sentence. He knows that the cancer is advanced. He knows not to say anything; he just listens.

I cut my morning classes the Monday after and explain to my counselors the news. I give one of my biology teachers a pass later in the week. She calls me over after class one day:

"Kayla, are you alright?"

"Yeah, I'm alright now." *No, I'm not.*

"Is somebody. hurting you?" *Not me, my father.*

"Oh, no, no. I, uh, found out my dad's sick a few days ago. I was upset."

"Oh, I'm sorry. Where is it?"

"Between the stomach and pancreas."

"My father died of pancreatic. It's really hard to see somebody go through it. Keep your head up. I hope he's okay, that it's not too advanced."

The summer is weird. Keeping busy is important. Working my first job, dabbling into running, enjoying the last moments with Danny as he prepares to head west for Pomona. Dad is in a more upbeat mood, as if his prognosis is a reason to keep living, something to fight for. He goes to treatments with my mom no problem. The only scares are the sketchy hallucinogenic painkillers the doctors are somewhat experimenting with. I start playing chess again for a little while, whenever he's up for it. He was the one that taught me years ago. We have the TV shows that we watch together, but he can never share the intense obsession I have with Walter White as I catch up with *Breaking Bad*. He refuses to see *50/50*, the epitome of a "dramedy." Anything cancer-related is too close to home for all of us, but I see past that. Cancer takes over the body; it doesn't have to take over the qualities of life that make life worth living.

Then Hurricane Sandy hits us, hard. The week is a blur. Power's out, no Internet connection, the basement's flooded. Dad's painkillers are running low, too low. Mom spends nine hours searching for a ride—any ride—in order to find a pharmacy that can give her the painkillers my dad is now addicted to. Time is precious, medication withdrawal not too far away. Chaos bombards us even more when the house becomes more and more unlivable as the toxic beach sand accumulates all over the floors and carpets. Uncle John houses us for a while, but he's housing other family members affected by the storm. There's a bit of tension. My uncle thinks I don't care about his sick brother because I seem preoccupied with other things. But all I can do is bring him what he needs and just ask him how he's doing. He's hard to talk to now. He's delirious. He can't eat. He wants to be left alone. After a week, I leave my family to stay with a friend for a few weeks. I do stop by once or twice to see how everyone's doing. Uncle John seems to be taking care of dad well. He and Mom are getting along better as well. I spend Thanksgiving with my mom's family, trying to develop a closer relationship with a cousin who's eleven years older. There's too much chaos now. I'm done applying for college, but I just want quiet. I want the bad things—the bad thoughts—to go away for a bit. The blur makes it bearable, until it goes away and I wake up and can't remember what has happened in the past month, except that my dad is still sick and my house and neighborhood will never be the same.

Anxiety creeps as I'm more and more out of the loop with my mom and the doctors on the state of Dad's health. I keep thinking about my eulogy for him, even if I don't want to. *What would I say about my dad?* Panic attacks strike anytime, anywhere, and anything triggers them. Concerned friends regret ever asking me how he is as they see me running away, hyperventilating and struggling to breathe. Class cuts accumulate, with guidance office passes to justify them. No teacher pulls me over to ask me what is happening. They assume "senioritis" is the culprit. The beginning of the end occurs when Dad refuses chemo in early February. It's too painful for him to handle. It's killing him. But that means he won't suffer for much longer. I have mixed feelings of loss and relief. Yeah, Dad won't live for much longer, but I won't get to see him in pain for much longer. I don't know what's worse, the physical stress cancer can bring somebody, or the emotional stress that it brings about on the family members watching their loved one in a pain that they have no control over.

Counselors try to get me to be proactive. One even has the audacity to "soften the blow."

"Kayla, what you're going through is tough and it's a part of life. But think of it this way: there are some kids who grow up without their fathers or have their fathers die when they're much younger. You've had your dad for *seventeen* years."

Yes, I'll still have the memories with him, the ones that will crush me and cripple my mind as I reminisce because I won't have all of the memories. He won't wave from the car window as he drops me off to college or give me away at my wedding or see my children or Nick's children. Am I supposed to feel selfish that I had my father for that long? I don't know if I should feel grateful or horrified. Well, what's worse, missing someone you've never known or having grown up with somebody you were so fond of who left the world before they were ready? All I know is that she is not going to be the only person to tell me this hard truth of life.

I forget that my dad is sick sometimes. It's as if he's gone to his bedridden states when depression took over his life when I was growing up. The only concern on my mind is if he had eaten. He's whittling down, looking more and more like a concentration camp victim with each passing day. It's frightening to see his body, and he knows it. He wears long pants and sweaters and rests under piles of blankets not only to keep warm, but also to conceal the damage the cancer has done to him. He's not getting better, but he's not getting worse. He has more days that he has enough energy to have conversations with me. It's nice talking to my dad. I tend to ask him questions about his past, because he's always been a private person. He seems to open up to me more, but in a very humble way. He tells me that he's lucky that I can take care of myself and that he's so worried about Nick. But that doesn't mean he stops worrying about me. He's worried about both of us. I tell him that Nick is the kind of person that will be okay no matter what he does. It's at that moment when I realize how terrified I am about leaving home for school in a few months. Mom is going to have a harder time taking care of Dad, no one else in the house to help her or be available to vent to during the crucial times. I won't know how Nick will handle everything.

The day we found out about hospice, I saw this look on Nick's face that I had never seen before—he was melancholic. There's no way of knowing how he's going to cope with this. Dad has always been his savior from video game addiction and the woes of middle school and high school. He was one of the few people that could get Nick out of the house, whether it would be to watch some crappy action summer blockbuster or to get a roast-beef sandwich at Brennan & Carr, probably talking about philosophy while they were together. I don't know what Nick's going to do without him. Nick has always lived to shock people, and the uncertainty of how he is going to cope really scares me.

I'm curious as to when the end is near. Hospice slowly comes into the picture within the next few weeks. I keep doing my own thing, thinking he's going to be in this state for a very long time. I start getting hours at a new job, the simple tasks that take up my shifts numbing my mind, keeping anxiety at bay and my mind at peace. As I go out with friends instead of staying at home, I feel twinges of guilt that aren't strong enough to keep me from going, but enough to keep from enjoying the outings to the fullest.

On a Sunday night in April, I feel lost. Something's not right. I have a tennis match Monday afternoon, but I have this itch to go to my support group, which is at the same time. My coach understands this and lets me go. The next morning as I kiss my dad's forehead goodbye, he's not responding the way he usually does. He usually wakes up to say goodbye before going back to sleep. I can tell he's reached a new point. He is mortal, and death isn't too far away. As I'm at the group, I start feeling anxious for no reason at all. I tell myself it's the coffee that I had right before I showed up. I tell Michele that Dad doesn't have very long. There are so many things I don't want to leave unsaid. I finally decide to apologize to him for all of the times I took him for granted. I didn't say thank-you enough to him. I made sure not to forget when I got home. Mom called shortly after group, telling me to come home. She sounded worried, but wouldn't tell me what's going on, someone's in trouble. I know it has something to do with Dad, but I don't want to think about that option right now. I call Nick and force it out of him.

"Dad's gone."

I pray that I misheard him the whole bus ride home. But I see my prayers will be forever unanswered as I see the funeral car and stretcher in front of my house. His lifeless body is left for me to say goodbye before he's carried away in a bag. I never got to say sorry. I take one last look at his blue eyes before I head to my room, wishing for sleep to wash over me, but it never does. The rest of the week was one of the most exhausting of my life. Sleeping is impossible, softened blows constantly being thrown at me by everyone I encounter. When I go back to school, I can no longer concentrate the way I used to, and I'm more frustrated with myself. Every day I fear that my concentration will be lost forever. My dad is no longer here to be my cheerleader, telling me that my hard work will pay off. Maybe he left when he did because he knew I was going to be okay from there. After his diagnosis, the first thing he said to my mom was, "I had a good life." He was ready to go a long time ago, and I like to think that he fought for the ones he loved, and I find that to be one of the most selfless things anyone has ever done for me.

Chapter 12

ALOHA MAHUAKINE: A STORY IN PICTURES

By Emma Burger

Or how my mom went from here:

to here:

And back here again:

I wish that this story were decades longer. I wish I could write a novel about my mom's life instead of a short story, but this is all I have. After she died, someone told me that "at least we still have pictures."

I can't imagine someone actually thinking this was of real comfort to a five-year-old who had just lost her mother. A photo can't take you to your first day of school or push you on the swings at the playground. A photo won't be there to sing to you on your birthdays, and you'd just look stupid if you tried singing to the photo on its birthday. You can't sit on a photo's lap, and it won't stroke your hair or call you Emma Kai-Lou and tell you that it loves you. Despite this, I'm so grateful now to the person who told me that then, because without these photos, I'm just not sure how much I would remember. In Kaui Hart Hemmings' novel *The Descendants*, a strikingly similar story about the life and death of a wife and mother of two girls in Hawaii, Scottie (the younger daughter in the family) makes a scrapbook of her mom as she is dying. Here is mine.

In 2000, my parents planned a trip to Hawaii. First we went to Honolulu in order for me and my sister to meet our great-grandmother Mama-san, and for my mom to unknowingly tell her grandma goodbye.

After staying in Honolulu with Mama-san for a few days, we got on a small airplane for our short flight to Kauai. We rented a house there for two weeks, right on Waimea Bay. This was where Mom showed us Hawaii: we went to the beaches, listened to the ukulele, ate shaved ice, tried in vain to hula without looking painfully white, and came out unscathed by the horrors of Hawaii's favorite mystery "meat," Spam. I could see that this was her place, her paradise.

In December of 2000, just months after our trip to paradise, my mom was diagnosed with non-Hodgkin's lymphoma, a cancer of the blood. I remember her saying one day that her stomach was killing her. She went to the doctor, and a couple days later we found out the diagnosis: turns out she was spot on when she said it was killing her. The next seven months were not easy. At first she was outpatient. She could still live at home but she would have to go in to the hospital and the cancer center. But she started going out less, wearing her pajamas more, taking a large collection of meds, and losing weight. She started chemo and refused to let it beat her, so she had my dad shave off all her hair before it could start falling out. They went into the kitchen with my dad's electric razor, and I peeked in as her dirty-blonde hair fell to the floor.

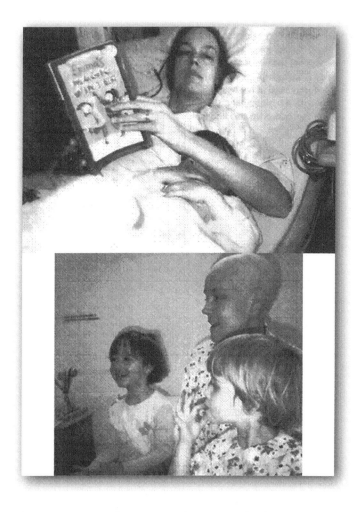

Once the chemo got more frequent and intense, she had to move to 16 East at St. Vincent's where she was receiving treatment, only really leaving briefly to go to the cancer center in the East Village. My sister and I went to Barrow Street Nursery School just a few blocks away from the hospital, and every day after school we would visit. That year, my grandma and great-aunt moved to New York to help. My sister and I had a fantastic babysitter, Lori, helping us, and so many of my mom's friends came to visit her.

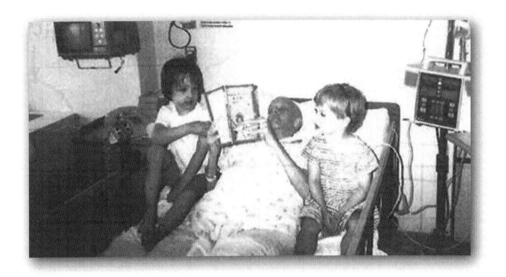

I think they kept it like this for my mom, but also in part for my sister and me. There were distractions all around the hospital. We would play games, Mom would read to us, the nurses brought us candy, and would walk around the floor with us. Mom was getting worse, chemo was draining her. The cancer was spreading, and although I never noticed, she was getting paler, weaker, skinnier, and more tired. We started to come twice a day, once after school and once in the evening right before bedtime, my sister and me in our pajamas. But still, everyone would say, "She'll be okay. She's a fighter."

One day, my dad and my grandma led me down the hall to a side room with a big table and chairs all around it. They told me to sit down, as if the weight of what they were about to say would knock me over. "Your mom is going to die," my grandma said. "But she might not!" I remember saying it over and over again until my face was red and everyone in the room was crying. "She might not, but she probably is," my dad said. But I didn't believe him, I couldn't believe him or it would be true. "But she probably won't! She might not die, she might not die, she might not die." I said it over and over again so I could know it was the truth. And then I buried my head in my dad's sweater and cried.

A few weeks later, it was mid-July and we were spending every spare minute in the hospital. My dad was sleeping there, although I have a feeling he was not really sleeping. Mom was making up for any lost sleep though, because that's almost all she could do at this point. But then one day, July 25th, we went to visit, and she became herself again. She was still tired, sick, and quieter, but there was a spark of energy in her. Naturally, I thought she was getting better.

I realize now that my dad was right. He knew the weight of what he was saying when he told everyone, "No, she won't be fine. She's going to die. We've taken her off the machines." The doctors stopped chemo and radiation, took her off the drugs, amped up the pain killer dosage, and were letting biology do its work.

On the morning of July 28th 2001, I woke up and knew that something wasn't right. I walked out of my room and went up to my great-aunt Sarah who was sleeping on an air mattress on the living room floor. "Where's Dad?" I asked, knowing that he had spent the night at the hospital. "He's in the shower," she told me. "Your mom died last night."

Everyone cried and cried, I cried out of profound sadness but also disbelief. We buried her in Truro on Cape Cod, our summer place. I missed her so, so much, but I couldn't bear to have anyone see me cry. At the funeral, I tried to hold it in. I preferred the pain of the lump in my throat to the pitying looks from everyone.

The next year, my family went back to Hawaii. We rented the house right next to the little one we rented on Waimea Bay less than two years earlier, back when everything was different. This house was much bigger though, enough to house uncles, aunts, grandparents and cousins. While we were there, we bought a lot of Iz CDs, a famous Hawaiian singer. One song of his, "Starting All Over Again," became our anthem. We played it everywhere, in the car, in the house; we sang it as we went about. In the intro, he says, "I was scared when I lost my muddah, my faddah, my brothah, my sistah, I was. But no, I guess it's something so weird, I'm not scared for myself, for dying, because we're Hawaiian, we live in both worlds. We can relate to this, we live on both sides. It's kind of like if I went now, that's alright. We cannot help it bra, it's in our veins. We cannot help it." We loved it because he was able to express what we were feeling. Hearing him say it in pidgin sounded so much better than it ever did in English.

When Hawaiians lose someone, they understand it. There's less blame; they grieve by celebrating the person's life. My mom was Hawaiian, okay only part-haole, but I cling to that because being in Hawaii, knowing that she is resting in paradise, gives me some comfort. I can go back to her by going back to Hawaii, or just celebrating the spirit of aloha. As I said before, a photo won't be there to sing to you on your birthdays, and you'd just look stupid if you tried singing to the photo on its birthday. You can't sit on a photo's lap, and it won't stroke your hair or call you Emma Kai-Lou, and tell you that it loves you. I feel Hawaiian and because my mom felt Hawaiian, I'll always have her. It's almost as if Iz is telling me that "She'll be there for the rest of your life. She'll be there on your birthdays, at Christmastime, when you get your period, when you graduate, have sex, when you marry, have children, when you die. She'll be there and she won't be there." Hawaiians are always talking about the spirit of aloha, and I think I finally know what they mean. Aloha means hello, goodbye, and love. It makes everything a lot easier, because it says all I have to say in just three syllables. Hello mom, goodbye mom, I love you: aloha mahuakine.

Chapter 13

AN INSPIRATION TO US ALL

By Jared May

My dad was diagnosed with stage three pancreatic cancer in January of 2009. The tumor was seven centimeters on his pancreas and surrounded his SMA artery. He was complaining of pain in his stomach for more than a year, and his doctors were not able to diagnose the problem. During that time he started looking at WebMD, a medical web site. Based on what he found, he thought he had pancreatic cancer and told his doctors. His doctors told him, "pancreatic cancer is an old man's disease; it's highly unlikely that you have it at such a young age." At the time, my dad was 48.

After many months of misdiagnosis, he finally had the right blood test in October of 2008. My dad was so frustrated at that point that he never followed up with the doctor. After literally waiting 4 months for the results, the doctor called him and informed him of what he already knew. One Year! A cancerous tumor on his pancreas had been growing for a year. Miraculously, it hadn't spread anywhere else.

At that point he began interviewing doctors for surgery. He was told that he was inoperable. One doctor said to him, "I am sorry to tell you that you are inoperable and if anyone tells you otherwise, they are lying." He went to more than three hospitals where he heard the same thing over and over. But he didn't give up. He kept fighting, hoping for a chance that one hospital would help him. Finally, he found one. Columbia Presbyterian in upper Manhattan agreed to perform surgery if the chemotherapy worked.

He started chemotherapy in February of 2009. His body reacted incredibly well to it, and though he was tired and weak from chemo, his resilience and strong mind kept him going. My dad maintained a positive attitude throughout. Finally, in October of 2009, they agreed to operate. The surgical team rerouted his SMA artery and took out part of his small intestine. The surgery went very well, and the doctors found no traces of cancer left after it. My family was ecstatic. His strong will and positive attitude had finally paid off. After more than two years it was finally over.

However, it was not meant to be. In September of 2010, his cancer came back. We were devastated. How could this have happened? This time around he had more complications. He developed headaches, cold sweats, and mouth sores from the chemotherapy. In March of 2011, he developed an abscess that wouldn't go away because his immune system was weakened by the chemo. In May 2011, he was diagnosed with an E. coli infection, and had to get a pick line in his arm to give himself intravenous antibiotics. He was in and out of the hospital every other week. Then, to try and drain the abscess, a stint was placed in his liver, but it didn't work, and had to be removed. In July, they found he had another abscess between his bladder and colon. In August, he had an intestinal blockage, and it turned out he had a parasite. In September, after he got rid of the parasite, he was put back on chemo. The following month, he developed a cyst, and had to get it drained. He also developed intestinal swelling, which wouldn't go away because of the chemo. There was literally one problem after another.

In January of 2008 my dad weighed 235 pounds; 4 years and 5 months later, he weighs 130 pounds. That's only five pounds more than me and I'm only fourteen. My dad is much weaker than he used to be, with much less energy, and there is one problem after the next. For all intents and purposes, he shouldn't be alive. And yet he is. Against all odds, he has survived.

From the time of diagnosis, the average pancreatic cancer patient lives 3-6 months. He has made it more than three years from diagnosis. My dad has an incredible will to keep going and to keep fighting. No matter how many problems he deals with, and no matter how sad it is, whether it's the cancer, or other infections, he maintains a positive attitude. He loves his life and his family, and doesn't want to give up.

He has set up a pancreatic cancer fund at Columbia to help others and has taught me many incredibly important lessons. Though it sounds cliché, I have seen it firsthand, in front of my eyes, for my entire teen-hood. No matter how hard life gets, and no matter how many problems you have, do not ever, ever give up. My dad is an incredible inspiration to me and should be to us all.

Chapter 14

IT WAS SOMETHING

By Joy Chiang Ling

When I was young I always thought that cancer was something I didn't have to worry about. I mean, sure, I heard about it on the news and read about it in magazine articles, but I never gave it a second thought because I didn't think it would affect me or the people I cared about. The reason why I thought this way was because I had an image of what cancer patients looked like: elderly people closing in on their deaths, pale anorexics with conspicuous veins, or hairless patients confined to hospital beds. Neither my loved ones nor I fit those profiles, so I continued to live blissfully unaware that cancer could strike my life at any surprising moment.

But as I grew older and my knowledge of the world expanded, I found out that the stereotypes I had in my head were only a small fraction of what the actual thing looked like. I soon realized that cancer could affect *anybody*, not just elderly people or patients in hospital beds. And I learned this not from a teacher or from a television special, but from watching the people around me get diagnosed with the illness one by one.

The first cancer patient I had the pleasure of meeting was a young boy named Ethan who I attended middle school with. He was a year younger than me, but had wisdom and experience more vast than my own.

He was a history geek who constantly preached about the virtues of communism, conducted geography competitions, discussed philosophy and politics, and engaged in intellectual debates. His appearance did not strike me as sickly at all, because although pale, his complexion was perfectly wholesome. Freckles dotted his face and red hair grew on his head and besides being relatively small statured, he was a normal, jubilant human being.

I always admired Ethan because he was incredibly bright and mature for his age, though sometimes I wondered if he had a dark side that he didn't want anybody to know about. The reason why I wondered this was because I would occasionally catch him whimpering in his bus seat or staring solemnly out the window, rather than explaining the intricacies of Marxism or listing the capitals of every European country.

It wasn't until a few months before my graduation that I discovered that he was actually a leukemia patient who had the disease since he was an infant.

"I'm very lucky I was one of the few people who survived," he said to me once with a smile, "because if I hadn't, then I wouldn't be blessed with the life I have right now."

To me, Ethan is a symbol of hope and triumph over the most uncertain of circumstances. Every time I think of it, his story conjures up images in my mind—images of a frail child struggling relentlessly against an enemy that threatened to kill him from the inside; of a child who fought and won, and lives to inspire others, including me.

Right now, I need this inspiration. I need encouragement and hope because at this moment I feel lost and confused in a world that's constantly changing and spiraling out of control. At this moment, I'm a teenager who's trying to become independent, trying to overcome obstacles and trying to mature into an adult. At this moment, I need a guide—someone to kick me to my senses if I go crazy and try to do anything stupid. After all, how could I remain sane when cancer continues to strike people closer and closer to me?

My struggle with cancer began when I found out that a family friend named Linda was diagnosed with bone cancer. She was the frail wife of a millionaire who constantly whined and complained about everything that crossed her path. Though she was hard to bear on occasion, I always seemed to feel sorry for her.

I remember a time when I was at a neighborhood block party. I went to Linda's house to clean my hands in her washroom, and after I finished my duty, she guided me over to her fish tank and talked about the "little fishies" that swam carelessly around in their artificial habitat.

"Your father told me that you would always get upset when a fish died," she said to me in her usual droning voice. "I get upset, too."

Her mention of my father and my pet fishes returned old memories to my mind—memories that I was always afraid to let go.

I suppose that is why I always felt upset whenever I thought about Linda's condition. She was one of the few remembrances I had of my childhood and of a long gone relationship I had with my father.

Fast-forward two years later. I am in a van, returning home from a therapy session I had in Chinatown.

My father is driving. It is one of those rare moments where I spend time with him alone. "Linda died a few days ago," he said to me.

"I know," I replied.

After an awkward silence, I ask him a question that's been nagging at my mind. "Did Linda say anything before she died?"

"Well, you know Linda. She's always pessimistic and complaining. Before she went into the surgery room all she did was whine. She just knew that she was gonna die and that was it."

She knew she was going to die. That seemed very typical of Linda—a cancer patient in the throes of her waking doom. Maybe her lack of perseverance was what led to her downfall, and maybe the exact opposite—the ambition to prosper—will save the lives of my two other friends who are struggling with cancer.

Just weeks after news of Linda's death had reached my ears, news of another cancer attack had reached my front door, and it was news that I found hard to swallow.

Another family friend named Annie was diagnosed with Stage II breast cancer on Christmas day, 2010. I always thought of her as the happy-go-lucky type—the kind of person that never loses hope and brightens the atmosphere when everything seems dour.

But that image I had of her tarnished when I saw her weeping about her condition in her bedroom. I listened to her stories about abuse and neglect and felt her many years of pain compiled into one narration. How could such a joyous woman break down in such a way? How could she break down knowing that there was so much hope in the world that could stave off her rapidly descending demise?

But Annie never capitulated. To this day, she undergoes treatment and receives the help of her family and friends. She continues to live with a smile on her face and an eagerness to survive another day.

Because of that, I admire her.

A few months after Annie was diagnosed with cancer, my mother confronted me about a lump in her breast. At first, I was in denial. I considered her discovery trivial and blocked out all of the negative thoughts I had in my head. There was *no* way it could be cancer.

But God smacked me in the face when my mom revealed her results to me. She really did have cancer.

From then on, I became withdrawn. I only told two of my closest friends about my worries because I was afraid that telling any more would make me an attention seeker. I tried to get the heavy feeling off my chest by talking to my social worker about it, but the appointment did little to relieve my pain. With nothing else to turn to, I resorted to doing what never failed to help me: writing. Thus, I began this essay.

There is a part of me that says I must not cry, that I must keep my cool and prove to my mom that I can survive without her being there for me. But another part of me says that it's ok to let out my emotions and show my mom that I care about her and that I'm afraid to see her go. But I'm afraid that crying means that I'm giving in to the bad thoughts that invade my psyche. Crying means that I'm being pessimistic and expressing a lack of faith. Crying means that my mom will not continue to live long enough to see me graduate from high school, graduate college, find a job at Pixar, read my published books in the bookstore, to witness my wedding and embrace her grandchildren.

But no matter how diligently I try to fight back tears, I'm afraid. When my mom told me that she had breast cancer, I didn't know how to react. I gave her the impression that I didn't care, when in reality I was trying to not show weakness. Right now, I just want to compensate for the years I've spent taking her for granted.

With the help of Annie, my family, our friends and me, I know that my mom will persevere. I have to remain vigilant. I have to work hard. I have to be positive. And, in the words of Ethan, I have to be happy that I'm "blessed with the life I have right now" because life—whether or not it is affected by cancer—is a blessing.

Chapter 15

MY GREATEST ACCOMPLISHMENT

By Chelsea De Jesus

My greatest accomplishment is not your typical thing to be proud of. So I would have to say my greatest accomplishment so far is making it through summer of '09. Unlike many, my summer was less than a vacation. Around the time of my 8th-grade graduation, my family and I found out that my father was diagnosed with liver cancer. Immediately my father's doctors ran dozens of tests to be sure the cancer hadn't spread to his lymph nodes. In mid-July we got back the results; he tested positive. That was a day I'll never forget. I don't think I've ever cried so much in my fourteen years of life. From that point on, you could see the toll the cancer was taking on him: his weight dropped drastically, he couldn't keep any food down because of the chemotherapy, and he was unable to go about his daily routine due to his fatigue and vertigo from all of the medication. For a while I just didn't want to think about it, and when friends of the family asked about my dad, I would just lie and say he was fine. To keep the guilt from settling in, I practically isolated myself from him, because if I looked at him for too long I would feel a lump in my throat. Once reality really set in I was able to admit to myself and others that, yes, my father has cancer. Then I found myself angry and frustrated a large portion of the time. I lost my patience with people so quickly that I found myself hurting people who were only trying to support me. During that time I also began to pray a little bit more, but I guess I was bargaining more than praying. For example, "God, if you help my father I promise I'll go to church more often." When my bargaining failed, I just didn't feel anything anymore, it was like I was simply numb. I didn't care about my appearance, what impression I left, or how I treated others. Underneath it all, I was still sad and angry but I just didn't show it. Then finally it clicked, in the midst of all my pain and suffering, I made other people miserable, too. At that moment I knew I needed to do some serious soul searching and on top of that an enormous amount of apologizing.

Once I finished with all of that, I began to realize that I had one of the most amazingly loving families a person could ever ask for. I would definitely say that I made it through this summer because of three specific reasons: my family, my friends, and my education. My family and friends gave me the love and support I needed, while my education gave me the drive to move on in life and to strive as far possible. If it weren't for those three things I would not have been able to make it through my first week of school with a stable mind. Luckily I have those three things, and I have a strong feeling that with a more optimistic outlook on life it'll make it easier to cope with what my father is going through right now. Overall I think what went on this summer and what is continuing now has made me a stronger person and in a way has prepared me for the real world.

Chapter 16

UNTITLED

By Kenneth Hicks

I was unsettled during the entire ride to the hospital. My mother had spent time in the hospital before, so I was not initially worried about her. However, I knew that she was not well when my uncle took me out of school early to bring me to her side. My uncle vaguely explained why he was driving me to the hospital, but I knew what was happening. I did not want to believe that my mother's illness had become too much for her to endure, but once I entered her room and saw several of my relatives crying, I was forced to face the reality of the situation. My mother's doctors told me that her cancer had spread to several parts of her body and that she would soon die. As I processed what was happening, I became overwhelmed by anger, sorrow, and confusion. These feelings consumed my mind and made me seriously question my future.

I received a lot of support from my family and friends, but nothing they said or did eased my mind. The first and most substantial feeling that came over me was the fear of living without my mother. My father died of a heart attack when I was two years old, so my mother had been the only person always present in my life. She taught me many things during my adolescence and was the person that I always turned to for support and advice. I was not sure if I could handle the obstacles in my life without her help. I knew that my mother would always help me get through my struggles. Without her, I no longer had the same sense of security, a new sensation that really scared me. My fear was accompanied by anger over how my mother's life was ending. My mother had fought cancer for three years with conviction. I hated the fact that after persevering through so much suffering, she still had to lose her life. I felt that my mother did not deserve to die because she lived so virtuously and so positively affected many people's lives. The fact that my mother was going to miss witnessing the rest of my life also angered me. Due to the absence of my father, I was extremely close to my mother. My mother loved me unconditionally and she always talked to me about how much she would enjoy watching me go to college, beginning a career, and starting a family. The fact that my mother was deprived of seeing in person how my life turned out seemed unjust to me. All of these feelings developed in me quickly and left me distraught.

Along with my emotions about my mother, concerns about my future also arose once I learned about her looming death. I was unsure of who I wanted to be my guardian. I had doubts about each relative that I thought could be my guardian and I was discouraged by the fact that none of them could provide me with the same life that I had with my mother. I also struggled with others' feelings. I knew that there would be family members who would be hurt if I did not choose them to be my guardian. I care deeply about my family members, so I did not want to hurt any of them. All of these factors made it difficult for me to choose a guardian. Another concern that I had was my future in school. I did not know how I would be able to focus on school when so many concerns were weighing down on my mind. Since I was a young child, I had always worked hard to succeed in school because I knew it would help me establish the life that I desire. I did not want my plans to be deterred by my mother's death, but this seemed very likely because of how much life would change once she died.

I struggled with many thoughts and emotions during the time of my mother's death, but I was able to cope with the loss and move forward with my life. I chose a friend of my family to be my guardian, a decision based on my desires rather than those of my relatives. I was also able to focus on school and maintain high grades in all of my classes. The pride that my mother took in my success inspired me to continue doing well. Most important, I established confidence in my ability to live without my mother. My mother taught me to never allow the obstacles in my life to defeat me. In her honor, I had to persevere and continue to pursue my aspirations, and believe in myself. As long as I do this, I can accomplish any of my goals.

Chapter 17

OUR NEW LIVES WITH CANCER

By Saloni Vishwakarma

Cancer has impacted my life. Throughout my childhood, I didn't know what cancer was nor did I understand what it did, until it affected me. Isn't that true about everything though? There's always something or someone in the world that brings suffering or is suffering, but we don't see how it matters to us until it affect us. Cancer has been a large part of my life and always will be. An illness, such as cancer, is like a ticking clock. Some have been saved by cures, however many have lost the war. Many people have fought the long battle with cancer, like brave warriors, such as my father.

In elementary school, it all began with one surgery. One brain tumor was the beginning of our new lives. At the age of 10, I was a little girl visiting my father in the hospital after a major brain surgery. Always seeing my hard working and energetic father with his head in bandages was too difficult for a 10-year-old to bear. To see my father sit on a hospital bed, surrounded by other patients was devastating. Still, the smile on my father's face didn't disappear. He was the man who would light up a room, and even at the hospital, that's what he did. He regained his health almost immediately and life returned to normal again. At home, he took multiple medications and I would make sure not to hurt his head or stitches whenever I sat with him. Every time he came home from work, I would run and give him a big hug. Life carried on normally for a year. I realized something was wrong again when the hugs became painful and he was not strong enough to lift his daughter. Slowly, things turned for the worse. Multiple times, my father went straight from work to the clinic and returned home with huge bandages. As his little girl, I would carefully get a scissor and help him remove the bandages. There were permanent marks of where the needle was always inserted. Still, I maintained my strength in front of him. Every time I saw the dark dots on his forearms, something pierced my heart, and I wished I could take away all his pain. If there was any way my father did not have to go through this and all his troubles could come to me. No longer did I want to see those bandages. No longer did I want to hear about appointments. No longer did I want to hear about hour-long MRIs. No longer did I want my father to go through this. As my father continued chemotherapy and medications, he began to lose his hair, and a blue cap became the symbol of my father's brain cancer. Everywhere he went, his blue cap went with him.

One day, just before entering middle school, my father came home wearing a hospital cap on his head. At that moment, something hit me. Something told me that what had taken my father to the operation room would take him again. I frantically asked my mother for an explanation of what was happening with my father, but nothing was known at the time. My father bravely decided to undergo surgery again. Again, now 11, the same girl visited her father in the gloomy, chilling hospital. This time, much weaker, my father lay on the hospital bed. As an 11-year-old girl, seeing her father in the hospital again after another major brain surgery, I couldn't hold it in, and tears flowed out like a waterfall. I couldn't watch him being taken away from me. Operation after operation, it had changed my father. Before, my father would donate every minute of his time to his work and his family. Now, another portion was made for the doctors. The doctors and the medications took him from me. As a young girl, I was eager to find out what had caused my father to go to the hospital twice. What had caused him to shave his head and wear that cap? What had caused him to grow weaker? But, whatever it did, it never took away his smile.

As my father's condition grew worse, nurses would come by to check his health and would always suggest guidance counseling to my family, but we always had each other. To cope, I would speak with my mom and my brother until late hours and write in my journal. My journal was full of compositions, poetry or sketches about how the day went by. Sometimes I felt that I was pulled underwater and cancer did not let me breathe. No matter how his condition grew, whenever you asked him how he felt, he would always say, "I'm feeling well." My father still bravely fought. My courageous warrior never gave up. He took breaths even after his lungs failed. He continued to smile even after his muscles stopped functioning. And I know that he kept his smile just for my family.

The impact of cancer has left an imprint on my life. My father's experience with cancer showed me how much he loved our family, since he would never wipe the smile off his face so that we couldn't feel his pain. From my experience with cancer, I have decided to become a neuro-oncologist when I grow up. These occurrences have guided me to grow interested in the study of the brain and how cancer forms within it. Having my father taken from me, I have grown determined to understand how cancer develops and to find its cure. Watching cancer affect my father day after day has instilled in me a determination and persistence to find the cure for brain cancer. Cancer has affected my life and always will as I continue to pursue my career to understand this deadly killer.

Chapter 18

ON THE SIDELINES

By Nina Leeds

Sometimes it is worse to be the one standing on the sidelines. You wish that you could just take the place of someone that is playing the game. You don't want to be just standing there helplessly. However, in my case, that is what happened. My mother was diagnosed with cancer when I was in kindergarten. I was very young, but it is a period of my life that I remember distinctly. Even though I was just a small child and did not understand exactly what was going on, I was smart enough to realize that something was not right. The moment that I remember most was the day that my mom had to cut off all of her hair. As a child, my favorite thing to do was play with my mother's long, beautiful, silky, blonde hair. I would twirl it this way and that, admire the effect if I put an alluring red ribbon in it, and make numerous braids. The day that she cut it off was the day that I realized that something was truly not right. I remember holding my mother's hand as I skipped into our neighbor's house; it was my neighbor who would be cutting her hair. I remember her sitting down in the chair and watching my neighbor timidly taking out the scissors. I remember the pang in my stomach as I watched her ponytail fall to the floor and just lie there, like sunlight glistening on the floor. I remember my sister running into the other room and I saw a tear fall down her cheek. She was older than I was and understood more of what was going on. I followed her, trying to look unperturbed. However, I could not hold back my own tears. As I scurried out of the room, I saw a tear trickle down my mother's face. This was the first time that I had ever seen her cry. As we left I knew that she did not know that I had seen her tear. I also knew not to bring it up. She left smiling, as she always did, a pink bandana that I would see for many days, wrapped around her head elegantly.

That is the one day that I remember perfectly. The rest really is a haze. I reconnected with my best friend that I had had in kindergarten, and we somehow got on the subject of it. I had not remembered telling anyone. However, she told me stories that I had told her that I could not for the life of me remember. Trying not to be rude, I responded as if I had remembered telling her this. I guess we really do block out the bad things in our life and try to remember the good times.

A while ago I read a book called *Autobiography of a Face*. This book described the life of a young girl who had cancer and it described, in explicit detail, her entire treatment process. I remember feeling sick to my stomach when I read about it and imagined my mother in that position. The thing that perturbed me most was how the protagonist in the book always talked about her being extremely weak during her treatment process. The funny thing is, I don't remember my mother once looking weak. I know she must have been tired, but the thing is, she never showed it. She managed to continue life with a smile on her face and never failed to come to every soccer game and every dance recital.

I also remember learning about cancer for the first time in biology. I had some basic knowledge of it, but never fully understood it. After learning about it, I realized how incredible my mother truly was. I remember the feeling I had when I was younger, during those times when I could sense her tiredness and sickness, that I would do anything to switch positions with her. My favorite game became Doctor. I would frolic around and bring my mother food and water and tell her to "eat and drink up." I would have my stethoscope in hand and would feel so strong and yet so helpless. It really was like watching your favorite sports team losing. You can't watch it; you would do anything to help them, but you're just standing on the sidelines.

Luckily for me, my story ends happily, unlike many others. My mother was cured and is now celebrating nine years cancer free. I still remember the first day that I realized that I could make a complete braid out of my mother's hair again. That day, I spent hours just running my hands through the beautiful hair. That is the thing about diseases like cancer. They affect everyone around you. Everyone feels what is going on, and everyone, in their own way, gets their own sense of completion. My mom received her sense of completion as she left the hospital after her final chemotherapy session. My sense of completion was making the braid again, just like old times. No matter what problem you are facing, if you give it time and remain strong, things can and will get better. I realize that I am incredibly lucky to have someone as strong as my mother to look up to. I never want to have to watch from the sidelines again, and I hope that nobody else has to either. However, for now, while a cure is still being searched for, the best thing that we can do is exactly what my mother did: keep a positive outlook and stay strong and carry on. It has really inspired me to try and make a change for the better. I have always done all in my power to help, including harvesting some of my own talents by doing "Runs/Walks for a Cure." When I'm older I hope that I can contribute even more to finding a cure. I do not plan on just standing on the sidelines ever again.

PART 3

BROTHERS, SISTERS, AND BFFS

Chapter 19

THE SIBLING STORY

By Sophia Capellini

My sister lost her leg to cancer at the age of seven. At the time, I was five. I thought her leg would grow back, but it never did. I also thought that my family would go back to the way it was before, but that never happened either. Instead, my family embarked on a journey of living a life quite different than those of my friends. It's a life in which stress occupies much of our time, but also a life in which every day is lived to its fullest. Cancer has certainly changed my family's life. Our family has grown closer, but cancer has also isolated us from other people who do not know what we go through. I can't imagine what my sister felt as she went through her cancer battle, but I do know how this experience has affected me.

When people hear stories of children with cancer, they obviously think of what the child went through, and usually sympathize with the parents, but they rarely take into consideration the effect it had on that child's siblings. Having a sister with cancer is not easy. Especially when you are five years old. It is hard to suddenly lose all the attention from your family in a matter of days. You're confused and angry and jealous. You feel ignored and constantly think to yourself, what did I do wrong? Why are they ignoring me? You then see your sister on a hospital bed, too weak to move, and slowly going bald, and you hate yourself for even considering getting mad at her. Then your family gets angry at you for demanding attention, and the vicious emotional cycle continues. It's hard to be forced to grow up and be on your own at such a young age, but under the circumstances, you really don't have a choice. When my sister got sick, my mother quit her job so that she could spend every day with her. My dad worked all the time, and when his shifts ended, he usually spent the rest of the day in my sister's hospital room. I spend most of my days at my grandparents' house. I slept there for many nights and sometimes went days without seeing my mom. I was upset and wished that she could spend more time with me.

My weekends were usually spent at Memorial Sloan Kettering, talking to my sister and meeting some of the friends she made in the hospital. They were all nice, beautiful and outgoing kids. It seemed like God had picked the best children in the world, and then cursed them with a deadly disease. Some of them were sicker than others. You could tell when you looked at them that they were too weak to walk without a walker, and didn't have the stomach to eat anything besides applesauce. Yet they all had smiles on their faces. They had hope that they were going to turn out fine; in fact, they were sure of it. Most of the time, it seemed like they were being strong for their parents, and instead of taking care of themselves, they were comforting their moms and dads. These children would have grown up to be great leaders and friends, but sadly, most of them were not as lucky as my sister. Relapse after relapse, they practically all passed away. It's incredible to even think that now, at seventeen years old, my sister has been to more wakes and funerals than most adults. The children that she had grown so close to, and that understood her better than anybody, had all been taken away from her by cancer.

Due to my sister's cancer, I've met some of the nicest, most selfless and positive people in the world. Happiness Is Camping is a summer sleep away camp in New Jersey. It is for kids with cancer and their siblings. When I was six and my sister was seven, we attended this camp, and I know now that it was probably one of the best decisions my family has ever made. While my sister met other kids who went through the same struggles she did, I met siblings who shared my feelings as well. At this camp we bonded with each other. We talked about our experiences and knew that we weren't being judged. I met counselors from around the world who planned on dedicating their lives to helping children with cancer. It was nice to be in a place where people didn't constantly point and stare at my sister's leg. They accepted her and they accepted me. Being at a sleep-away camp also made my own bond with my sister grow stronger. Without my parents around, she relied on me to help her with anything she needed. From holding her bags as we walked around the campus, to getting her food during meal times, and to even helping her hop into the shower at night. I was able to better understand what exactly she went through on a day-to-day basis. This, I know, has helped me become a better and more supportive sister.

Cancer has taught my family valuable lessons. We've learned not to take anything for granted and to live everyday like it is our last. Because, for some people, it is. My mother constantly tells my sister and me to do everything we can and never pass up an opportunity. Now that I look back on it, I don't really remember a life before my sister got cancer. I've grown used to a life of using handicapped passes, making frequent visits to the hospital, and even having birthday parties for my sister's "little leg." When I look at my sister, I don't think about her missing leg. In fact, sometimes I even forget about it. Even though I see her as a regular person, a lot of people don't. Many people look at my sister and don't know what to say or how to act around her. They think they might offend her somehow and think that because she has one leg, she has different feelings and personalities than they do. I hope that people will realize that even though she is physically different, she is still like any other girl. She talks, and laughs, and jokes like we all do. She stresses over what clothes to wear, worries about school, and watches *Law & Order: SVU* reruns just like the rest of us do. However, having cancer has made my sister braver, stronger, and more courageous than anyone I know.

Even though cancer has made my family's life hard, it has inspired us to start living our dreams today. We've seen, firsthand, how precious life is and how quickly it can be taken away from you. Today, my sister doesn't give up on anything. She spends her winters skiing with other amputees and spends her summers rock-climbing. She recently went on a service trip with her school to Cambodia and enjoyed every minute of it because she was helping others. This fall she will be attending Johns Hopkins, where she will be going pre-med. Her dream is to become a pediatric oncologist and help other children with cancer. Because of my sister, I've learned strength, perseverance and most of all, love. I've learned to love myself and love others, because everybody's life is valuable and worth living. Sadly, the physical effects of my sister's cancer will be with her for the rest of her life. However, the valuable lessons my family has learned from this experience will also stay with us and help us all become strong, daring, and fearless.

Chapter 20

THE STRONGEST MOTHER

By Erica Galluscio

In almost every romantic comedy I've seen, the protagonist is a girly, hopeless romantic with a somewhat less-feminine best friend. The best friend is usually a neighbor that symbolizes the main character's tougher side. Luckily, my childhood idol, Faith, and I fit these roles. Growing up across the street from each other, Faith, her brother Will, and I were inseparable. We played every day after school, even though I went to a public school and they went to a Catholic school. Naturally, my mother and their mother, Teresa, were close as well. Their family was large and not typical. Inside the small house across the street lived Teresa, Elizabeth, Jackie, Laura, Faith, and Will, age descending respectively. The father figure was not much of a father figure to the kids. He was completely out of the picture and, from what I've been allowed to hear, he was and/or is an alcoholic. Their house was infamous on the block; it was the house of loud music at late hours, and screaming matches that could be heard from miles away. As the children grew up, police cars were often parked outside their house, too.

Still, I knew who my best friends were and I didn't care what the neighbors said about them. But when I was too young to understand, or to even be informed of the situation, when Faith was 4 and Will was 3, Teresa was diagnosed with cancer. If I knew more about the situation, I would say so, but I knew very little at the time and I know very little even today. I have memories of my parents conversing about it behind closed doors. I remember the words *bone marrow, transplant,* and *blood transfusion*. I know what they mean now, but it never made sense to me at the time. I also have brief memories of seeing Teresa without hair, or with a neck brace. I know this didn't last long, because as I grow up I often forget it ever happened. But whenever I say something like "Didn't it go away at one point?" Adults are always quick to correct that. "No; it never went into remission." I hear that a lot, I guess.

I always knew Faith's home life was bad and, as we grew up, we grew apart. I became smarter and I found myself. I was the geeky, childish girl with equally childish friends. I studied and read a lot. On the weekends I watched old movies. At night I watched cult-following TV shows. But Faith lost interest in a lot of things about which she used to be passionate. Really, she lost interest in life, or at least it looked as such from my perspective. I could only watch from afar as she deteriorated, as she belittled the potential she had by befriending older and dumber kids. She was such a bright little girl; she was mischievous, too. I was warned not to follow the path she was destined to take. I didn't understand at first, but now I do. Adults would always say, "Of course she turned out like this, just look at the family." But I refused to believe it was more than a phase. The phase turned out to be more of a lifestyle. By now the adults' words had become so hurtful that I stopped listening.

All this was over a course of 13 years. I'm 14 now, and about 9 months ago everything changed. Suddenly, Teresa was weaker than she had been in a very long time. My mom and Teresa were sitting on the lawn chairs in my front yard; I decided to join them. From what I heard, Teresa had been advised to move in with her sister and sell the house, just to ensure that the two youngest kids had a place to live in the long run. I only remember one quote from the conversation, "I don't want to sell the house and move, because I feel like that's giving up." Teresa's hair was thin and grey, she needed a cane to move around, she could no longer do yard work, and she didn't feel like giving up.

I couldn't go a day without talking about it. I got as much information as I could from my mom. I started sitting with them whenever they got together to talk or have tea, but it seemed as if nothing was happening.

I thought so until I saw the "For Sale" sign.

It had finally happened. The infamous house was destined to be emptied and sold. The entire family was gone in less than a month, even though no final sale had gone through and the house wasn't clear of furniture. I never even got a goodbye from the girl I grew up with. I guess I didn't deserve one, with me not trying to save her all those years. I carry this burden with me always. I was always complimented for my maturity and questioned for my choice of remaining her friend. I, of course, grew to believe that I could have somehow showed her the way when she needed it most. I think I still believe that. Why did I back away from her when she began to go astray? Were the words of the grownups too scary for me to ignore? Did I really believe that speaking to my childhood sister would somehow infect me with a false disease that was no more than a cry for help and attention? I think about this quite often. What could I have done?

My mother, the woman with the biggest heart for everyone but herself, went into the house daily to help clean it up—removing bags of garbage at a time. I was helping her one night when Spike, the family cat, sauntered out of a vacant bedroom. His angry yellow eyes were large and gleamed in the moonlight that streamed in from an open window. His glossy black fur shined, and I remembered the day he was brought to the neighborhood almost 10 years ago. He cried faintly, desperately even. We later discovered that Spike was supposedly left on his own, seeming capable of forging for food for himself. I refused to let that happen. I scooped the small thing into my arms and determinedly carried him into my house, leaving my mom to continue cleaning. There was no arguing; we were going to keep him.

Teresa and the two youngest kids had arranged to stay at their aunt's house. My mom visited almost every night, and I didn't. But I tried to pretend like I was helping by asking my mom how her visits went.

Teresa was getting worse and the kids were miserable; it was the same up-date every week. We invited the kids over as often as we could and, when they did come over, we tried to act like how we did in the old days.

It was another one of those nights. Faith, Will, my dad, and I were around the table playing a board game. My mother quickly paced into the room with a phone pressed to her ear. As she chattered to whoever was on the other side of the call, she motioned for us to get up and get our jackets. We all knew what was happening.

It happened quickly; it seemed that in under a minute we were all in my mom's car discussing what was going on. She didn't know much except that Teresa was in hospice, something I didn't know, and that things were "getting bad" according to her nurse.

⊰⊱

The drive to the hospital was a solemn one.

Nobody said much, we just listened to the rain pound against the windows. It was a low, muffled sound from the inside. I liked the sound, so I concentrated on that instead of the impending tragedy. My mom haphazardly parked the car, and silently we trotted to the hospital doors. Faith and Will knew the way to their mother's room, so my mom and I followed in haste.

I had never been more shocked in my life. I had only seen her twice in the past month, but within two weeks Teresa had deteriorated incredibly. Pale, thin, fragile, wrinkled, worn. This was not the strongest mother of five who battled cancer and still managed to do manual labor around the house. This was just another victim of cancer, which, from my perspective, took away everything Teresa was but her illness-stricken body. The tears appeared at the corners of my eyes, but refused to fall. Faith and Will took their respective seats around her bed, and I found one on my own. Faith put her arm around me for the first time in years.

"You okay?" she whispered with a smile.

I blinked, stunned, and the tears vanished. It took me a second to realize the irony of who was asking whom that question.

"Fine, but what about you?" I said it softly, and I couldn't smile. My mouth was still hanging open from the shock of seeing what was left of her mother and hearing Faith's cool tone.

She giggled softly and turned back to the bed. Then I cried.

⸻

From 6:30 to 9:00 we sat silently. Occasionally new people joined our party and occasionally people left. Nobody really knew what we were waiting for, or whether we were waiting for anything at all. Faith and Will had left the room for a little with Jackie. I was alone with Teresa, Laura, who was holding Teresa's hand, and one of Teresa's nephews.

I started counting her breaths. I watched Teresa's pale chest rise and fall, far slower than my own. I tried to match my breathing to hers, but I couldn't do it. It was just too slow to be comfortable; I felt like I was choking then saving myself over and over. I counted about 30 and realized it was pointless; I was just entertaining myself. Then her chest heaved, and I snapped to attention. It heaved again; I stood slowly, watching.

Then blood. It was just blood. Her neck seized forward and her stomach convulsed quickly, forcing a long, thick stream of dark blood to gush from her mouth. Her nephew remained calm and rushed to her attention; Laura and I looked at each other and ran from the room searching for help. I dashed through the hall looking for a nurse. If I didn't find one, I knew Teresa would die.

"Excuse me!" I shouted the second I saw one at a desk. She jumped, startled from me shouting at her. I hurriedly explained the situation, hysterically motioning towards the direction of Teresa's room.

The nurse slowly removed her glasses and put a hand up. "Calm down. I'll come."

I watched in horror as she took her time. I was sure Teresa was dead now and that it was my fault. My head whipped around; I didn't have time for this. I sprinted back to Teresa's room, the tears stinging in my eyes. I just remember feeling frustration and pure adrenalin. At that time, I was positive that I hated nurses. I hated hospitals. I hated doctors. I was convinced that they view everyone as the same. Death is common. They don't care who lives and who dies. They didn't know Teresa, or her family, or her story, or her legacy, or me.

⊰⊱

I wasn't allowed in Teresa's room; a nurse had gotten there already and was attending to her. I was relieved, but a bit disappointed. I wanted to see her; I wanted Faith and Will to see her. But we were rushed out and urged to go home.

We reluctantly left. I had nightmares of throwing up blood and dying that night, and I woke up tired and scared the next day.

It was 5th period. I had a class called Studio Art. I had been checking my phone compulsively throughout the day.

The text message read, "Erica its will she passed."

I darted from the classroom and down the stairs, pausing on the stairwell between the second and third floors to cry.

The funeral was the following Saturday. At it, I made this speech:

"The greatest thing about Teresa was how she made you feel. You could walk into her house at any time and feel like a welcomed guest. She'd invite you to sit down and talk, but she'd never talk about herself. She was always interested in how you were doing. Even when she was sick and weak, you could ask her how she was and the worst you would ever get was 'a little under the weather.' Teresa made you feel like you mattered because you were able to make her day."

Chapter 21

ONE DREADFUL THING

By Alicia Romeo

ancer. That rotten word. Have you ever felt the pain of losing someone you love to cancer? I have. *Thingy* was his favorite word. I remember the first time I laid eyes on Anthony, he was wearing Sketcher sneakers. They were orange, blue and grey. This one moment was in third grade. I only started talking to him at the end of third grade. We became Grade A friends. We had the greatest times with each other; I never thought that would all end one day. I and many others adored Anthony. He acted like nothing was wrong. He never showed any signs of having cancer. The beginning of fourth grade is when the cancer started to act up. He had a puffy face, chubby cheeks. In my eyes all I saw was a boy that I admired. Whenever he was around the days seemed brighter, but that all ended once I lost him. I felt as if a huge storm cloud came rolling over me and followed me wherever I dragged my slugged mind. I can still see those brown, brown eyes in the back of my mind, sparkling in the sun. The middle of fourth grade is all a blur except for December 5th, 2007. The morning of the 5th of December 2007 was like any other normal day. I woke up, got ready for school, and left for school. I noticed something out of the ordinary, Anthony wasn't there. As the day drew near to the end, I went to visit him. All I remember is standing and watching in awe. I looked around and saw others standing around, giving flowers to his parents. He was just lying there in bed so motionless, as if he were a waveless ocean. The cancer had spread all around his tiny little body. He could not move at all because of this beastly disease! I keep forever in my mind the moment I walked next to him and took his hand, and told him that he was my best friend in the whole wide world. When I spoke to him, his eyes looked like they began to have life in them again. This moment in time keeps playing in my mind over and over and over again as if it were a movie that you watch over again and again because it was so good. I have always wondered till this day why he opened his eyes so wide when I spoke to him, and I will wonder this forever and ever. On December 5th, 2007, 7:29, my finest pal had died all because of this senseless cancer. On the morning of the next day, which was a Thursday, my mom told me that Anthony had passed away. In that second, I never ever, ever, ever thought... that I lost my best friend.

From my experience with cancer, I would say that I learned that even if you want that person to stay in your life, when it's their time to leave, they must go.

Chapter 22

THE CONTRADICTIONS OF CANCER

By Emily Marcus

Cancer presented me with a series of contradictions, a reevaluation of words and their meanings. Although I had previously thought of myself as rather private and unemotional, I was forced to reassess my feelings and gain more sensitivity when my brother was diagnosed with Ewing's sarcoma early last year. As much as my experience felt so raw and real, so, too, did it feel impossible and surreal. And, as much as I watched my brother mature, so, too, did I painfully see him rewind the clock back to his days of youthful vulnerability. These contradictions have led me to realize that my experience with cancer was a confusing one; it cannot be defined by a single word or event. And, to this day, it is something that I am still struggling to fully comprehend.

I wouldn't exactly consider myself a sensitive person, harsh as that may sound. Yet, when my brother was diagnosed with cancer the summer before my sophomore year in high school, I felt a need to challenge this facet of my identity. Why was I unable to cry when my mother told me that my brother had a malignant tumor on his pelvis? Why did I never show my feelings about it around my friends and family? Why was it that whenever my guidance counselor called me in to discuss it, I always dodged his questions and ended up talking about school instead? And why was I so desperate to pretend that nothing was wrong and that everything had remained the same?

I've concluded that this emotional confusion was caused by the surrealism of the whole situation, as overly joyous as that word may sound. And here is one of the ways that the idea of contradiction and reevaluation comes into play: cancer has made me question what reality and surrealism really entail. Usually used to describe magical fantasies or dreams, the word "surreal" also seemed to fit my life at the time. Yet, it took on new meaning. I remember when my mother told me about my brother's tumor, it seemed impossible. I remember telling my friends that my brother had cancer, and I remember them periodically asking me how he was doing. I remember replying vaguely, quickly, nervously—as if I could not find the words to express myself, or at least they clung onto my tongue, unwilling to dive into the vacant, daunting air. I remember visiting him in the hospital, having to quickly give up my fear of needles as I watched him get more shots in one day than I had endured in my lifetime.

In a way, this experience was as close to reality as I had ever come in my life. This was raw, unadulterated pain, fear, and suffering. Yet, it was also the most surreal, illusory experience I had ever had. When I would sleep at the hospital with my brother, as much as it was a rude awakening to see small children in the pediatric wing of Memorial Sloan Kettering Cancer Center—walking around looking sickly, emaciated, tired, with IVs in their arms, bandanas on the heads, and dark black circles drooping beneath their eyes—it was also surreal. Not in the good sense, of course, but in the bizarre one. My life took on new meaning; it assumed a new identity. I felt as though I were living in two disparate worlds. Spending the night in my brother's hospital room on weekends, although almost unbearable at times, also sort of seemed like a fun activity; it was a sleepover with my brother whom I had missed while he was away at college. We'd order in Chinese food, watch movies, and play board games. This was the surrealism of childhood; it was the imaginative, juvenile side of things.

This surreal youthfulness constantly presented itself, yet it was not always so jubilant. My brother, who was twenty and the oldest kid in the family, had so quickly and shockingly become the youngest. He was on a floor with more babies than adults, sharing a room with a boy five years younger than I was. My mother was forced to wipe him when he defecated, as if he were a baby. And, when he came home after chemotherapy, he often lay on the couch whining like a young child. We helped him when he puked, we nurtured him when he had a headache, and we fed him when he needed to eat. And, after his grueling, 10-hour surgery, we watched him take his *first* steps for the *second* time in his life.

Yet, despite this childlike defenselessness, I have never seen someone quite as mature as my brother. As cliché or even as senseless as it may sound, it takes a lot of *maturity* to return to a state of *immaturity*. My brother was forced to accept being rapidly pushed into this position of helplessness. It was not *his* choice to be wheelchair-prone or neutropenic. Yet, for me, this caused a role reversal.

This is where yet another reevaluation comes into play: what is the significance of older and younger? Suddenly, after years of being the baby of the family, I was home alone and left to fend for myself. Day after day I returned from school, arriving to no one, or to a single parent who was exhausted from a night at the hospital followed by a full shift at work. I remember when I had mononucleosis and was home sick for three weeks, practically alone. This proved the helplessness that cancer forced not only on my brother, but on my family as a whole. I lay in bed, helpless, as I could not gain the energy to move or work. My brother also lay in bed, helpless because of what cancer had done to his body. And my parents felt helpless, too, unable to provide each of their children with the necessary attention and care that they so desperately desired.

And so, cancer caused confusion and reevaluation in my life. I thought about the meaning and presence of sensitivity and feeling, of reality and pain, and of age and growth. I watched as these things so quickly transformed, spinning my whole world along with them. Yet, realizing that these definitions are so easily challenged by cancer has made me comprehend the true magnitude of my experience and the importance of life and perseverance above all else. While attending a stressful school and dealing with the college process, it is often difficult to remember the lessons that cancer has taught me. It is all too easy to get caught up in the pressure of school, worrying about a test score without realizing that there are far graver issues facing our world. Yet, it is because of these reevaluations and contradictions that I have been able to gain *perspective*. Although I am still working tirelessly to piece together my experience, I have realized that, as much as cancer has made me focus more *specifically* on my brother's health, it has also allowed me to consider my decisions and actions more *generally*, and in a much larger context. It is hard to find justification, reason, or explanation for something so seemingly unfair and incontrollable. I do not know if I will ever be able to fully make sense of cancer; yet, I do not know if *anyone* is truly able to do so.

Chapter 23

THE UNBREAKABLE BOND

By Bryce Cammarata

Dealing with cancer is a relatively new experience to me, but over the last four years, I have begun to see the threat it really is. My best friend Mark was diagnosed with brain cancer when he was only 12 years old. Shortly after his diagnosis, he went to the hospital to have surgery to remove the tumor on his brain. Mark was extremely lucky that the tumor was caught sooner rather than later. Even though the surgery was successful, Mark had a few side effects to his tumor. Mark's left arm has grown weaker, along with his left leg. He has developed a limp and needs to work with a physical therapist frequently. He has been working on building up the strength to use his left arm just the same as his right arm.

When I first met Mark, I was unaware of his condition and formulated my own ideas on what his disability really was. Me and Mark were buddies but didn't talk as frequently as we do now. A year went by from freshman year, and I became one of Mark's best friends. We talked about everything; he told me what his disability was and what his recovery process has been like. I learned so much about how badly cancer affected him and his family.

Mark has annual check-ups with the surgeons to check on his recovery process and they check him to see if any cancer is growing back. There are many things Mark can't do because of the damage caused by the brain tumor, and it makes him sad sometimes when he sees the enjoyment other people have. Mark was able to play guitar before his surgery, but now he can't until his hand is built up to its full potential. For the three years of our friendship, I discovered what fun we can have without him feeling bad about his disability. Many people don't play board games anymore because they seem boring or frustrating, but we have the greatest time of our lives playing them. Our favorite game to play is Quelf. It's one of the most outrageous board games out there. We play this game and have enormous amounts of fun acting out silly actions the cards ask us to do. Besides board games, we sit and listen to music. We both love and compare singers and musicians and debate on who is the best and who isn't. We make the most fun out of the simplest things we have. Sometimes we stay up all night making milkshakes and cooking pancakes when we are hungry.

Every year when Mark is checked for cancer, he gets nervous and afraid of what the outcome will be. The last seven years that he has gone, he has been cancer free. Mark puts a lot of stress and pressure on himself about many things in his life. I have been there to make him feel comfortable in public, in school and anywhere else we go. I try to ease his mind as much as I can because he can't handle all the stress built up inside of him; it's hard for him to talk about his feelings sometimes. Recently he was diagnosed with Crohn's disease, which has been taking a tremendous toll on him. His diet changed to a very limited selection of food that he can eat without making him sick and running to the bathroom every couple of minutes. Recently we went to Applebee's, and Mark ordered the dragon fire steak without realizing how spicy it was. We stopped him before the waitress left and told him how bad it was for his stomach. He had to change his meal to salmon with steamed broccoli. When dessert time came around, a couple of our friends got dessert, but Mark couldn't have any. I felt bad and sacrificed my dessert and didn't order any with him so that he didn't feel left out or alone.

I have never left his side and never will. We are best friends till the end, and I know what my best friend needs and how to make him happy. Whether we play Quelf until we can't laugh any more or we rock out so hard that our necks hurt, we have the most fun making the most of what we have. Mark may be limited by his physical abilities on some activities we would like to do together, but our friendship will never be limited. I will always be with Mark, building our friendship closer and closer every day. Along our journey to adulthood, we will discover new activities that will give us the fun and excitement that we love to encounter.

Chapter 24

THE RIPPLE EFFECT

By Marcus Thomas

Cancer victimizes more people than those directly affected by it. It finds a way to victimize anybody connected to the men and women whom it directly affects. This is the ripple effect of cancer, and the way by which I came to know about and experience its potentially life-changing effects. Let me explain where I'm coming from with this metaphor. I never had cancer, and nobody in my immediate family has ever had cancer. I came to know its effects from the mother of my half-brother, a valiant woman named Sharon Thomas. Given Sharon's relationship (or past relationship) with my father, I never got to know her very well. I knew that she was the mother of my half-brother Darryl, I knew that she used to be married to my father, and I knew that she held Secret Santa parties at her house that my family and I used to attend when I was a child. This was why, when I learned that she had been diagnosed with pancreatic cancer, I was more worried than I was devastated. The most reprehensible, disgusting part of my worries was that they weren't for Sharon, but rather for Darryl. These sentiments, along with my outlook on life, would shift later on due to ripple effect. The ripple effect would not only change my life, but bring me to mourn over a woman whom, although a family member, I barely knew.

Because of the timeline of the events that transpired in and between my father's two marriages (Darryl's mother and my mother), my half-brother Darryl is much older than I am and lives very far away from me and my family, in North Carolina to be exact. Consequently, we talk to each other fairly often, but rarely get to see each other, so when we do, we spend time together in good spirits and good humor. Therefore, this was the only side of him that I had ever known; the good-natured, funny side, and I liked this side, this person whom I thought was Darryl. So when I heard that his mother had been diagnosed with pancreatic cancer, I had absolutely no idea how he would react. There was no doubt in my mind that he was taking it worse than I was, but I just couldn't picture him in mourning, in a state where his aura that I liked so much disappeared. The months went by, and Darryl and our father regularly visited Sharon at the hospital. Based on what I heard when our father reported back about her condition, Sharon never gave up the fight or showed any hint of despondence. She battled cancer until there was no will or strength left, and there was plenty to begin with. The effect that this losing battle with cancer had on our father was painfully clear to everybody in my family. Sometimes when he returned home from visiting Sharon at the hospital, he would just sit down, mumble about Sharon's worsening condition, and then just remain pensive and introverted for the rest of the day. Even though I wanted to know, I just couldn't gather the courage to call Darryl and ask how he was doing. This was because I didn't want to see another side of him. I had become so accustomed and attached to his humorous side that I couldn't and wouldn't face the reality that he was going through a tough time. I didn't want to get to know the other side of him, the human side, and the side that felt pain. As the condition reports got shorter, more repetitive, and more depressing, everyone in my family knew that the battle was lost. At this point, I stopped being worried and started being scared, this time for Sharon. The realities of cancer-related deaths were foreign to me at the time; I only knew what I saw and heard in the media. Although I knew that the parallels to real-life cancer-related deaths were minimal, I couldn't stop resigning myself to that knowledge and that horrible imagery every time I thought of her. I feared the worst and imagined all possible outcomes. Then, on April 20, 2010, Sharon Thomas died from pancreatic cancer.

The effects on my parents, especially my father, were immediate and obvious; they were definitely hurt by Sharon's death. As I said before, I did not know Sharon that well so the effects that her death had on me were less severe at the time. The life-changing effects came later, through an alternative vessel. This alternative vessel was none other than Darryl, the same Darryl whom I worried about earlier and the same Darryl of whom I only wanted to see the better side. After his mother's death, I desperately wanted to extend my consolations to him, but for the aforementioned reasons, I couldn't and wouldn't do so. All it took was a slight prompt by my mother for me to contact him to offer my consolations. When he responded was when that slow, metaphoric ripple touched me. His exact words were, "Thanks, bro, remember to cherish your own mother." This response set in motion, for me, the closest a 15-year old could come to a midlife crisis. I began to ask myself questions that we human beings don't like to ask ourselves. Questions like, "Am I really cherishing the people that are important to me in life? If I died tomorrow, who would care? What would I be remembered for?" And, most important, "What could it possibly be like to battle with cancer? For death to become a daily reality? To waste away with my loved ones as an audience, and to subject them to such grief as I and everyone around me are feeling now?" The answers to these questions brought me to an epiphany; I was missing an essential part of the human puzzle. I was not loving and cherishing the people in my life with as much fervor as I could. I realized that this was not only cold, but it was not what God had ordained for me, or for anybody, man or beast. We were given the ability to love and cherish, and I was squandering it away on material, temporal things instead of extending it towards people. As was my habit, I deduced these things and suffered in silence, trying to improve myself and, in general, love more. To this day, I still struggle with this, but the death of Sharon Thomas serves as a brutal motivation and reminder of why I need to cherish those in my life, especially my mother, while I still have her.

So that's how cancer's devastating ripple passed through my half-brother, through my parents, and reached me. That's how Sharon Thomas's cancer changed my life. When one really stops and thinks about the metaphoric ripple effect of cancer, it builds in strength, the metaphor that is. A network of people (friends, relatives, students, teachers, etc.) is like a body of water, held together by bonds of varying strength. Whenever there is a disturbance in this otherwise tranquil body of water, or a tragedy in this otherwise peaceful, friendly network of people (in this case, cancer), there is a ripple. This ripple will spread, first with its greatest, most forceful intensity to the water molecules closest to the source of the disturbance, just as the cancer of a loved one will have the greatest impact on those most closely related to him/her. This ripple will lessen in strength as it spends more time in the body of water, and therefore, it will touch other molecules with less force, or the impact isn't felt as strongly in distant relatives/friends. So I have been somewhat enlightened, even while mourning, as a result of Sharon Thomas' cancer and subsequent tragic death. I know, by the metaphor, that this ripple either passes through me with less strength or ends with me. However, through this essay, I hope to share the facts of the devastating effects of cancer on a network of people (community, neighborhood, friends, etc.) and defy this metaphor I've expounded. This ripple will go through me with more strength than with which it came, it will reach more people than it meant to, and by all the power that I can put into my words, the victimizations of cancer will be made clearer than ever before. Thank you for hearing my story.

Chapter 25

INDELIBLE

By Annie Fan

The walk to York Avenue from the subway is a long one, so it gives me lots of thinking time. Often during this walk in particular, a young girl comes to mind. She dances and sings in front of a video camera. The strands of her hair twirl and weave gracefully through the wind, her eyes coyly smile along with her lips, dancing charismatically.

I've watched this in my mind so many times. The video is grainy, and the audio mediocre at best. Sometimes, the sound falls out of sync and her lips mouth to nonexistent music. The tousled windblown hair is stimulated with a rusty old house fan. The video is shot on a Sony Handycam from the 90s, and the girl in the video is my five-year-old sister, Amy.

Fast forward three springs later. Amy is eight. The hair that once moved so gloriously in the wind is gone. She is bedridden, the music replaced by monotonous beeps emitted by IV monitors demanding attention. The setting is Minneapolis, Minnesota, the only place that they would administer the experimental chemotherapy treatment after all other options at Memorial Sloan Kettering had been exhausted. But this time it's different. This is not a video. This is my life, and everything is a just a little too real.

The next memories that flooded into my mind were the darkest ones I've ever known. They were memories that pierced through the mind like a deep, visceral pain. I remembered the night Mom, Dad and I left the hospital close to midnight, numb, quiet, carrying suitcases full of clothing, toys and books that had once been Amy's. Amy did not leave with us tonight. She had fought valiantly for almost four years, but she had lost and she was gone. So we drove home together in silence with tears streaming down each of our faces in warm rivulets, illuminated by the linear street lamps on the highway. Yes, I remember the night of July 22nd; I remember the funeral, the elaborate casket, adorned with richly ornate and oddly resplendent flowers. Amy loved life to its fullest and bright colors, so when the florist told us to opt for white roses symbolizing childhood innocence, we chose not to. It was a beautiful July day when a row of cars somberly followed the hearse through the gates of Flushing Cemetery.

Now I am taken back to the present. I put on an ID badge as I near my destination on York Avenue. It indicates my position as a child-life volunteer at Memorial Sloan Kettering Cancer Center.

The journey I made with my sister during her life defines my life today. How could it not? There Amy was in her hospital room, propped up against pillows with a ridiculously heavy bucket full of candies she had just obtained from the Friday night hospital candy cart. She'd grinned deviously at me whispering, "Aren't we lucky?" I smiled weakly, trying to hide my disagreement. Of course, we weren't lucky. We were different. Where other siblings had discord, we had love. What other people took for granted, we treasured. We had learned to value time like we never had before, living, celebrating the simple fact of being alive—together.

There Amy was again, a few days after her bone marrow transplant assuring me that she was not in pain when she saw my face contort in concern. Throughout her treatment, Amy only exuded strength, never self-pity. The spirit that Amy embodied during her life was alive in me, and now I would share it with many others. Her willpower remains beautifully contagious. And finally, there she was again nearing the end of her battle, with a breathing mask that could only be removed for brief moments. It took a few moments before I could make out what she was saying between her quick shallow breaths. "I love my sister."

The familiar elevator ride to the ninth floor sets my mind racing again with memories. There she was again in that silly homemade music video. The video is grainy, and the audio mediocre at best, but it is a beautiful moment.

PART 4

MY FAMILY

Chapter 26

NANA

By Emily Friedman

When my mother was seven months pregnant with my older sister, four years before I was born, my 62-year-old grandfather passed away from a sudden heart attack. As my nana and my parents left the emergency room to return home, my father told Nana she shouldn't be alone, and that she should stay at our house for a few days. A few days turned into ten years because shortly after my birth, my mother returned to work. Since Nana was still living with us, she became my primary caretaker and a second mother. We were together every day, and as soon as I graduated from a crib to a regular bed, I snuck into her bedroom almost every night. I would fall asleep in her arms, with my head nestled into her chest. There was no more comforting place in the world. Nana supported me in everything I did, and I could always hear her voice above all other noise and clamor, screaming my name. Although my parents were often mortified, I was never embarrassed in the slightest. I was shy, and she gave me the confidence to persevere.

When I was eight years old, my older half-brother came to live with us, so Nana moved into an apartment about ten minutes from our home. Although technically she wasn't living with us anymore, she still had dinner at our house nearly every night, and often slept over. When she wasn't at our house, I was at hers. She usually slept on my pull-out bed, and we would fall asleep holding hands. She was an incredibly loud snorer, and every time it woke me up I would tug her hand. She would stop snoring for about ten seconds, before resuming snoring even louder.

Whenever the hardships of grade or middle school seemed overwhelming, she held me while I cried, no matter how silly the reason. I'll always remember the feeling of her warm, calloused hands as she smoothed my hair back and did everything she could to make me smile.

There was never a dull moment with Nana because she had a heart and personality as large as the sun. The endless adventures we had together could fill a book. One of the more frightening and exciting adventures that we laughed about for years was when we were on our way to pick up Chinese food and my nana made a wrong turn and ended up on the tracks of the Long Island Railroad. Nana was incredibly stubborn and insisted she could maneuver the car off the tracks. It took me 10 minutes to convince her that she couldn't back the car off and it was only a matter of time before a train would appear. A couple of big men came over and tried to push the car off, but it wouldn't budge. Eventually the police and fire department arrived, we were both questioned by detectives, the car was lifted off the tracks with a crane, and we drove off, after Nana charmed the police. My mother, on the other hand, had a conniption.

When Nana was 79, she was diagnosed with uterine cancer. We were all cautiously optimistic because she had beaten colon cancer nearly 20 years earlier. Nana underwent surgery to remove the cancer, but because there were positive lymph nodes she needed postoperative chemotherapy. Nana's cancer turned out to be so aggressive that she ultimately underwent three sickening and painful rounds of chemotherapy, the second of which involved an experimental drug that seemed to make her sicker than the disease itself. On one occasion my mom let me go with her and Nana to a chemotherapy session. The thing I remember most was the awful smell. Although I wasn't allowed in the treatment room, I remember sitting outside on a stool with my nose crinkled in disgust. The room reeked of sorrow and chemicals, and the melancholy pall was unbearable. It was at that moment, as poison dripped into Nana's bloodstream, that I finally realized the severity of her illness. Nana recognized the severity as well, especially when none of the toxic drugs the doctors gave her worked, but she didn't show it, nor did she never lose her courage or sense of humor. One of the drugs Nana received gave her uncontrollable diarrhea, and my mom and I had to take her to a lab to get her stool tested for bacteria. While most people would have been filled with shame, Nana continually joked about the contented look on her face after she eliminated. She made me laugh until I had tears in my eyes and a sore stomach.

After her final round of chemotherapy, Nana's cancer progressed relentlessly. It eventually spread throughout her abdomen and into her lungs. It was hard to imagine that anything could be stronger than Nana, but she became so weak that she had to move into our house once again. Only this time it wasn't for her to take care of me, but for me to take care of her. As her condition deteriorated, our living room slowly became a hospital room, complete with an oxygen tank, a hospital bed, a sequential circulator to prevent more blood clots in her legs, a walker, a wheelchair, a commode (which Nana refused to use until the end), and a small pharmacy for all the drugs she had to take. My parents and I helped nana with everyday tasks like getting her up to walk to the bathroom, getting her in and out of bed, washing her, feeding her, and making sure she was as comfortable as possible.

On February 20, 2013, I spent the entire night in my room hysterically crying - great, heaving, uncontrollable sobs - as I listened to Nana's desperate pleas for pain relief. The next morning I lost my best friend. Every time my phone rings, I think it's Nana, only to realize it can't be. My iPhone, which Nana bought for my fourteenth birthday, is now part curse as well because it's filled with pictures and videos of her. My voicemail is full of messages from her, which still leave me grief-stricken.

I wish Nana could have been with us for 10 years again, but this time it was only for four months. Watching her deteriorate was the hardest things I have done, and ever will do. During the last few weeks of her life, our main concern was making sure she was in as little pain as possible. She was on oral narcotics and special patches to help ease the pain, and she was delirious much of the time. I sat with her every night, and we held hands as we watched *Family Feud, Judge Judy,* or *Wheel of Fortune*—her favorite shows.

I've been told there are five stages of grief: denial, anger, bargaining, depression, and acceptance. There must be something wrong with me because I'm going through the first four all at once. I don't think I'll ever experience the fifth stage because I cannot fathom ever accepting that my nana is no longer with me, but that is only because she still is with me. Almost everything I see, do, or hear reminds me of her in some way. The fifth stage for me will always be confusion.

Last year my parents took me to see the play "Shadowlands." It is based upon the life of the Irish writer C.S. Lewis, who is best known for *The Chronicles of Narnia.* The focus of the play is Lewis's meeting with an American admirer, Joy Gresham, whom he befriends and eventually marries. "Shadowlands" deals with the tremendous love Lewis felt for his wife and how he never imagined he was capable of such intense emotion. It also deals with the terrible pain and sorrow that Lewis had to deal with after his wife died from cancer. At one point in the play, when it is clear that Lewis's wife is dying, he asked her: "Why love if losing hurts so much?" to which Joy responded: "We can't have the happiness of yesterday without the pain of today. That's the deal."

So that's what I keep telling myself: I had a good deal because I got to grow up bathed in love from the most magnificent, courageous, funny, and loving person I will ever know. I am so incredibly lucky to have had someone like her in my life, and although I am suffering, I am happy that she isn't. Not a waking hour goes by that I don't think about my nana and miss her desperately. A cruel disease has stolen her from me, and left me in tatters. Without Nana here to knit me back together, I am submerged in a pool of anguish, desperately trying to breach the surface.

Chapter 27

A YELLOW BRACELET

By Caitlin Rubin

My mother used to keep a yellow bracelet in the top drawer of a white desk. The bracelet was made of rubber—the stretchy kind that drags along your skin as you pull it on—and it was worn down; it took a special light to see the letters that had since been smoothed by anxious fingers. The desk was nothing special. We didn't even use it. Wads of envelopes and crumpled papers bulged from the space between the desk and drawer and tilted back the spindly chair and heart-shaped pillow that guarded it. A peg-board rested on the wall behind it-dog-eared, off-white clippings and old photographs on its surface—an old man, an inspirational quote; the desk had many friends. I used to pass that desk every day; read the quotes; look at the pictures. I would lean my arms on that brown wisp of a chair and rock back and forth, reading those words and trying to match the people I saw in those photographs with the blurry ones I saw in my head.

My mother got the yellow bracelet when I was eleven years old. My grandpa gave it to her. I knew nothing about that bracelet then. I knew the capitals of all fifty states; I knew the difference between Mesopotamia and Sumeria;

I knew which one was the Tigris, and which the Euphrates; I knew what a cumulus cloud was.

I did not know that my grandpa was dying of cancer.

I don't remember when I found out. I don't remember what it felt like at the time. But I do remember that my brother was away at college, and I was sitting in his room watching the Disney Channel on his TV when I heard my dad call up from downstairs. Naturally, I was annoyed to be drawn from my show, but I could tell that he was serious about something or other, and I hopped up. I remember wondering if I was in trouble.

When I turned into the kitchen downstairs, I saw my sister with her face buried in her hands. Her cheeks were red and her brown hair ringed around her face in a messy swirl like one of those cumulus clouds I knew so much about. I distinctly remember my dad as he turned his head to face me and said, "It's over." Truthfully, I didn't know what was going on, or what exactly was over, but my dad was quiet and my sister was crying, so I started crying, too. It seemed appropriate.

"Grandpa's died." I don't remember who it was that spoke the words, just that they were spoken. I felt sad, but I didn't understand. I just sat there and cried and watched my big sister and my dad because they seemed to know what to do.

We went upstate for the burial, and I sat and played with my cousins in the funeral parlor. I noticed the flowers and the people dressed in black—all drawn to the big brown box where my grandpa was. He looked asleep to me.

My mom and aunt came up to me and said, "It's okay to be sad. It's okay to cry." I felt like they expected that of me, so I cried. I still didn't understand. To me, Grandpa was going to be sitting in his recliner at the next Fourth of July picnic, wondering why people had made such a fuss.

As it got later and people trickled out, my mother and aunt were there again. They looked tired. Something struck me in the way the parlor's dimmed lights pulled shadows from beneath their eyes. I looked to my grandpa laying in his box, and something changed about the way I felt then—I truly realized that would be the last time I would ever see him.

There was something so significant in that moment for me. I was young, conditioned to expect "firsts" from my world, not "lasts." I cried then, really cried. For the first time, I felt sadness that was my own, not an imitation of those around me. It did not feel appropriate, it felt personal, and I didn't like the panic that overtook me then.

On October 29th of last year, Hurricane Sandy hit my hometown of Long Beach, NY. As residents of an island, my family and I were used to the evacuations and bridge closings associated with hurricanes. We dug and dragged a hundred and fifty sandbags over from the beach, locked the doors, grabbed the dogs and escaped to Westchester County to wait it out. I walked through my kitchen one last time before we left and got a feeling that things were about to change.

For seven days, we shivered in the cold, waited on gas lines, played far too many games of Scrabble, and worried whether or not our house had made it through the storm. Again, I found myself in the same state of disbelief: wandering through the days, worrying when school would start up again, crowding into the few coffee shops and nail places that still had power and heat. Again, my stupor was broken roughly; we opened the door of our home only to see water and mud pour out at our feet. Everything on the bottom floor had been covered in a combination of sewage, oil, and seawater; you couldn't stay in the house for over an hour before the fumes gave you a headache.

Together, my mother and I cleaned and packed away everything salvageable on the bottom floor. We dried seawater from photo albums of trips to Disneyland and VCR tapes of first steps and dance recitals; my mother found her wedding dress soaked in the hall closet.

In the corner of the kitchen, my mother's white desk stood with a watermark three-quarters of the way up its side. We dreaded what we would find when we opened the drawer. My grandfather's picture hung over the desk, untouched by the flood. Inside, my mother's bracelet sat in the miraculously dry drawer, the same bright yellow color, the same letters still faintly carved out on the side. Amidst all the wreckage, that bracelet had survived. We survived.

My mother now keeps her yellow bracelet in a new drawer, inside our new temporary apartment. She picks out flooring and doorframes and tile and wears those letters down a little more each day. I am sure many people own that bracelet; I'm sure they're handed out at fundraisers and lost in the car. To my mother, that bracelet is special; it holds a small piece of my grandfather inside of it, a piece of his strength—a strength she passes down to me each day. My grandpa doesn't sit in his recliner at the Fourth of July picnic anymore. Instead, he sits in all our hearts, and in that little yellow bracelet that my mother used to keep in the top drawer of her white desk.

Chapter 28

UNCLE SANTA

By Rachel Rigodon

The first time I met Uncle Adler, I was about six years old. My mother had been prepping me a few hours before, instructing me to be on my best behavior because a guest was coming: her brother-in-law.

So of course, I sat at the table politely, waiting for the stranger to come in, upend the household for a while by making us use the nice china and guilt-tripping me into saying that I remembered him when I really didn't.

I smelled him before I saw him. He smelled like special occasions. Of course, now that I'm older I recognize that smell as rum and cigar smoke. He was tall and round with soft white hair and red cheeks and nose. He looked like Santa Claus.

And he was loud. Either from telling a joke or from laughing or from asking, "Who is this beautiful little girl? Val? Wow!" He grabbed me, and my head was pressed into his soft, wide belly that was twice as big as me and always arrived first wherever he went.

I loved that smell, and the way he didn't try to make me talk. Instead he was content with keeping me on his lap and laughing with my father, his warm sweet breath always heavy with the Barbancourt Rum that my parents always bought at the airport. I loved his fat red cheeks and the glasses that were perched above his coal black eyes. He was a great storyteller, the kind that got everyone laughing and talking, but still listening to him. I loved the way he caught everyone's attention in a way I knew I never could, even at six. If he was the life of the party, then I was the little spirit hovering over his shoulder.

The next time I heard about Uncle Adler, I was eleven years old. The first things that popped into my head were red cheeks and rum.

"You remember Adler?" My mom had asked. "He has esophageal cancer. He's not doing too well, so we're going visit him. You want to come?"

I nodded, and prepped myself for medical mode. My mother worked in a hospital, so I wasn't nervous around sick people. From what I knew, they usually sat in hospital beds with the TV on some fuzzy channel and the remote hidden somewhere. They would speak to my parents while I sat and tried to figure out why *The Simpsons* was in Spanish. The patient always looked tired, but other than that fine.

Instead, we drove to an apartment complex and went up to the fifth floor. I let my hand travel across the banister that separated me from a long and grisly drop to the sidewalk below.

The green door opened, and my mother and aunts and I filed into the darkened apartment. A woman I didn't know talked, and I wondered how well Uncle Adler was doing. If he was back home, it must not have been that serious.

One by one, they all went into a room in the back and then returned stern and sober. Uncle Adler was in that room, and soon it would be my turn to go in and talk, though I didn't know about what.

The room was not big. The shades were drawn, and a tall white lamp in the corner shed an ethereal glow across the long hospital bed and IV lines placed in the middle of the coarse dark blue carpet.

And in the middle of that bed was a skeleton. Uncle Adler was no longer fat or red or jovial. His face was gaunt, and his skin was ashen and yellow. I stood near the door and watched the man in the bed. He wasn't moving, but his dark eyes were open. This wasn't right. Sick people belonged in hospitals, not in their homes. There were no doctors at home. There were no surgeons at home. There was no hope at home.

From my spot in the corner I peered at him, the little spirit once again but this time without a life to watch. I didn't want to go near him, but I did. If just to make sure that if he could see anything, he saw me. He smiled creakily, but he couldn't talk because of the plastic blue tube attached to his neck. He was wearing a diaper, and several tubes and wires were attached to his frail body. I was horrified. This was cancer? How did it escape from the health book and into my life? All those times I had heard about the dangers of cigarettes and alcohol, whether in class or on the TV, could never have prepared me for seeing him like that. It was all that rum. The bright red in his cheeks that had reminded me of Santa Claus, now told me that he was a chronic drunk. All the laughing and drinking, which had seemed exciting and festive now seemed disgustingly excessive and destructive. He knew this was going to happen. I know he had been warned about his habits thousands of times, and yet continued to do what he was doing. *He knew* and he let this happen. I wondered whether he thought it was worth it. If all those years of storytelling were worth having to spend his last months in a diaper, never feeling the sun again. Having to face the little spirit who was angrily judging him for purposely killing her uncle.

After a few minutes, we left. For some reason, I remember the sun setting vividly. It was a bright orange and red that painted the sky beautifully, and it stung my eyes. I kept my squinted eyes on the sun, but kept away from the edge of the walkway, and we drove back home.

The last time I heard of Uncle Adler, he was dead. When I thought of him, I saw the skeleton again and smelled urine and bleach and hopelessness. We weren't going to his funeral, because it was being held in Haiti. And even if it was being held in my backyard, I wouldn't have wanted to go. The more time I spent remembering moments like those, the less space I would have for Uncle Adler, and his cheeks, and his smell.

These are things that I will never get back. These are things I will never give up to skeletons, or funerals or time. They are my memories of a Santa Claus alive and laughing, telling stories, and smelling wonderful, and asking who that beautiful young woman is.

Chapter 29

ALWAYS IN MY HEART

By Ryan Markoe

My Aunt Andrea was a strong, athletic, loving person. She was vibrant and full of life. In August of 2008, she passed away after a two-year battle with brain cancer. I have a special place in my heart for her. Although she is not physically here, she will always be a part of my life.

I love being involved in sports. I have played soccer, basketball and golf since I was five years old. My Aunt Andrea also loved competing in sports, and her favorite sport was volleyball. She was a high school all-star and had a very successful college career. Being physically fit and healthy were important aspects in her life. She passed this onto her three children as well as her nieces and nephews. Since I was the oldest of her nephews, we developed a special bond.

Every summer my Aunt Andrea and Uncle Donald would run a two-week basketball camp. It was always something to look forward to at the end of the school year. It was so much fun learning new dribbling and shooting drills, defense and, of course, to look forward to the end of the school year. It was even better because I was with my older sister, Kristen, and my six cousins. Every morning we would get up at seven o'clock to eat breakfast.

Each morning my Aunt Andrea would make something different for us to eat. We had pancakes, waffles, French toast, sausage, eggs and bacon. At the same time she was making breakfast, she would ask the cousins what kind of sandwich we would like for lunch. It was fun to watch her make peanut butter and jelly sandwiches, ham sandwiches and, of course, my favorite, rolled up bologna with no bread. Every day she would ask me, "Ryan, are you sure that's how you want it?" and every day I would say, "Yep, that's it."

During the day at camp, she was always making sure I was enjoying myself and telling me to drink more water. One of my favorite things was during lunch. She would sit with me and teach me to stretch. She would explain in great detail the importance of stretching and how it could improve my game. I loved getting the special attention from her but I found stretching to be boring. However, now, before each game that I play in, I will stretch for thirty minutes to get my muscles warmed up and ready to compete. I can still hear her voice telling me what to do. It brings back such a good memory I shared with my Aunt Andrea.

After the day at camp, we would go back to the house and swim in the pool for hours. My Aunt Andrea would sit and watch us. She would be the judge when we had our diving contests.

Unfortunately, all of this changed after she was diagnosed with brain cancer. At first everything she did seemed to be the same. However, as time passed, my Aunt Andrea, the person who I always knew as vibrant and full of life, was now struggling to live. It was very difficult for me to watch how she became less and less involved in the basketball camp and at home. Watching my Aunt Andrea looking at her three children and knowing that she was not going to be able to help them and watch them grow left me crushed. As this debilitating disease progressed, it was incredible to witness all the responsibilities that were left for her three children and my uncle to carry out. She was unable to work at the camp, and I really missed our lunchtime stretching sessions. This was always a special time for her and me and now it was gone. I was so upset. She would try to make breakfast, but would get annoyed because she could not remember what she was doing. One of the worst days for me was when she could not remember my name. I could not believe she did not know my name. I felt so sad. I just wanted to cry. She could not make our lunches anymore. It was so heartbreaking to watch all of the cousins making their own lunches. Try to picture eight children in the kitchen trying to make their own lunch. It was a disaster. I really miss watching Aunt Andrea make our lunches.

The basketball camp in the summer of 2008 was the most difficult for me. My Aunt Andrea was unable to get out of bed. It was heart wrenching to see her physical appearance deteriorate. My sister could not go in to see Aunt Andrea because of the way she looked. Kristen said it was scary for her to just say hello. My sister would cry and be visibly upset just thinking about what Aunt Andrea was going through. I wanted to be strong for my sister. As hard it was, I forced myself to say good morning and hug Aunt Andrea every day that I was there.

The day that she died, I was playing golf with my dad. When he answered his phone, I knew at that moment my favorite aunt had passed away. My Aunt Andrea showed me incredible strength and willpower in the face of adversity. She taught me about perseverance, hard work and determination.

Each year on the anniversary of her death, my family and I write notes on index cards, attach them to balloons and let them fly into the sky. It is a great way for me to remember my Aunt Andrea and the special place I have in my heart for her.

This summer will be third year without my Aunt Andrea at the basketball camp. I know she would be so proud of me. I am now an instructor at the camp. I am the person helping young children improve their basketball skills. I am the one showing the campers how to stretch. Yes, I know she would be proud. Do you know how I know this? This past Christmas my uncle gave me a letter my Aunt Andrea had written while she was sick. In the letter she told me what an amazing young person I was and how proud she was of me. She was the amazing person. Even in death my Aunt Andrea continues to have a tremendous impact on my life. I will never forget her. I love her and miss her so much.

Chapter 30

THANK YOU

By Hannah Chi

Although I've known many people in my life who have experienced or dealt with cancer, the person who has impacted me the most is my grandfather. Although his death was both painful and regretful, it also opened my eyes and it taught me many things. Although I would like to say that I had an ideal relationship with my grandparents, I cannot. I never had those simple, cinematic memories, such as baking cookies with them or listening to their old stories about the wars they've fought in or the mountains they've climbed. My grandparents and I live across the country from one another; they are situated in California while I live in New York. I saw my grandfather three times in my entire life during family reunions, and those memories were still not as joyful as I would like to remember them. This is partly due to a speech barrier between us, because I am more comfortable speaking English while he can only speak Korean.

Three years ago, when I was still in 8th grade, my family got an urgent call and, before I knew it, we were on an airplane to California. I told my teachers that it was a family emergency at the time, but I really had no idea what was going on, except that my grandfather had lung cancer and it had spread.

I remember seeing my grandfather in the intensive care unit, unable to talk and move. He was barely able to breathe, and that was only due to the many fluids and machines he was hooked onto. It's a life-changing experience to see someone you care about say that he wished he was dead.

In a span of a week during my visit to California, my grandfather went from the hospital bed to a cemetery. I saw how my dad was fighting and struggling to stay strong in front of us, how my uncle was pressured by the fact that it was his decision to either pay the money for my grandfather's cancer medication or cut his air supply, and how my grandmother was utterly broken down. My older brother and I tried to stay calm and take care of my younger cousins. My grandfather took a part from each one of us.

My grandfather's death filled me with a guilt I couldn't comprehend. I only had a few memories of him, and I realized that I didn't know him at all and that I never really tried. I always look through my family albums now, and I appreciate pictures and the value they have in inspiring reminiscence. My grandfather's death also brought my family closer together and made our reunions dearer. Now I treasure the moments I call my grandmother, and I try to make her laugh, although she cries every day. I want to thank my grandfather for the faith he has given me, and the ways he made me realize that I need to cherish and love the people I have now.

Chapter 31

THE EMOTIONAL ROLLERCOASTER

By Jack Bellear

We spent the past ten months in a never-ending chain of rising hope and then having that hope shut down in a flash. We were all riding an emotional roller coaster that no one wanted to be on. My family and I slowly regained our strength while swinging in and out of denial and wondering when the pain and suffering was going to stop. Though we all knew the unfortunate truth of cancer and its effect on people, we would try to find ways of disbelief and prayer just to keep a small glimpse of hope alive. Beginning in November, the months passed, the seasons changed, and the tunnel of light for my terminally ill grandmother slowly became brighter and brighter.

Every hospital visit was a mind game, and every phone call, whether it was from a hospital, a nursing home, or even Grandma herself, made all of our hearts skip a beat. Personally, I hated going to the hospital to visit. Of course it was nothing against my Grandma, but just the fear of seeing her hooked up to oxygen tanks, a needle in her arm with an IV tube running through it, and seeing the look of anguish and exhaustion on her brittle face killed me. She had developed cancer in her spine, and somehow, every time we went to visit her at the hospital, she looked and acted better than most of the patients I saw on the way in.

The hospital is to this day my least favorite place on earth. My dad had told me to just try not to look in the other rooms as we walked from hallway to hallway to get to Grandma's room, but that was almost impossible. Left and right there was the dreadful atmosphere surrounding me, every room had an old man or old woman who had a downhearted look on their face, and they too had large machinery hooked up to them to keep them stable and alive. But the worst of it was the nauseating stench of death and disease that was all around everyone. The smell of hospital food and the horrible aroma of the people that laid on the hospital beds in dismay seeped up my nose and straight into my brain. Finally, when we would get to Grandma's room, the sad truth was unveiled. She looked just like anyone else that was laying there looking for anything to distract them from their thoughts. She would put on a fake smile and a cheerful mask to try and let my brother and me know that things would be okay. As I looked around the room she was in, it quickly made my stomach turn. There were small cans of Sprite and bottles of water that were half-drunk, uneaten food that the hospital had given her, but mostly candy wrappers and cookie boxes that were brought over from my other relatives on other occasions. I would find myself just sitting around, my stomach aching, and it occurred to me that my Grandmother was doing most of the talking. Grandma, the selfless person that she is, would make conversation with my brother and me and ask us how we were doing. Essentially, every visit to the hospital resulted in my grandmother wondering how we were doing and putting none of the focus on herself. Although it was comforting to see her acting energetic and outgoing like she used to be, every hospital trip resulted in melancholy by the time we all left. As the months passed, Grandma lost all of her hair from the treatments she was being given. A couple of times she was permitted to go back home, but then just when you think things were finally starting to settle down, she was headed right back to the hospital again.

Eventually, in July, she was moved to a nursing home and things remained constant for a little while. The visits there were not as bad as the ones to the hospital, although the sight of people in their eighties with Alzheimer's and dementia and all other kinds of brain diseases was still very creepy. She spent all of her hours lying on a bed, watching television and sleeping almost all hours of the day. I noticed that over time she became quieter. She would lose her breath quickly during every conversation, and it seemed she was becoming weaker and weaker. My father went to visit her every single day since the very beginning, and I noticed that he, too, was becoming almost depressed after going there so often. Summer ended, and school began, and after just a few weeks of school, Grandma was back to the hospital again. The daily sickness in my stomach came right back, and this time, it seemed to me that this would be Grandma's last trip to the hospital.

A week went by, and on a Wednesday afternoon in the beginning of September, I mustered up the courage to go visit her in the hospital. My mentality going in was that this could be the last time I ever see my grandmother, so I had to make this visit special for her. When my father, my brother and I walked into the hospital room, we had to put on these plastic anti-germ smocks to prevent any germs at all from getting near my Grandma. My heart stopped for a second when we walked into the room. All alone, my once outgoing, energetic, loving and overall happy grandmother was lying unconscious on what I presumed would be her deathbed. She was hooked up to an IV tube, an oxygen tank and a mask over her mouth, and a feeding tube going into her stomach. Seeing her in such agony and pain horrified me. When my dad woke her up, I saw a smile appear on her face, she was overjoyed to see her grandsons. She couldn't talk much; I found myself forcing small talk knowing that I would only get a smile back or a muttered, "Yeah." She was completely bald and she could hardly move her arms, though she battled the pain just to hold my hand. Under the sleeve of her hospital gown I noticed several bruises, due to the fact that she stopped developing platelets and there was no longer any protection from bruising. Her upper arm looked similar to a Slim Jim, it was pure red and shriveled up like a sun dried tomato. Her hands were black and blue with bruising all over, and she could hardly find the strength to smile, though she did. We only stayed for about thirty minutes, and when I kissed her goodbye, I was sure that it would be the last time I would see her.

On the way home by brother burst into tears, as did my dad after seeing him. I sat in the passenger seat, emotionless and still in shock. I began to wonder why I was not crying, too.

When we got home that night, I tried to eat some dinner and watch the Yankees with my dad. I could not stop thinking about what I had just saw, and at about ten o'clock that night, my dad got a phone call from my uncle, who was begging him to come to the hospital immediately. My dad got off the phone with tears streaming down his face, and said to me that Grandma was having trouble breathing. He told me he did not know when he would be home, and from the second he walked out the door, all I could think was "Is this it?" or "Is this going to be the end?" For two hours I sat on the couch with my thoughts, not knowing what to do or say, but I was almost hopeful that it would just be over for her already. When my dad finally arrived home, he had told us that she was okay, and the doctors operated on her to fix her breathing struggles. There was a sense of relief, but also a sense of deflation, due to the fact that they were just prolonging the suffering. On the way to school the next morning, my dad had told me they put a breathing tube down her throat to take her breaths for her. He said that the plan was to gradually increase her breathing ability to the point where they do not need the tube anymore, but he and I both knew that there was a very, very slim chance of that happening. The thought of what she could have looked like still haunts me, I envisioned it as her just lying there unconscious with a huge tube holding her mouth open, making a lot of noise keeping her alive and taking every last breath for her. She could no longer breathe, she could no longer eat; she was living off of machines. At that point, I did not even want them to bother anymore; I just wanted this whole grueling process to be over. My dad had agreed with me, but he told me something that somehow made me feel a little better. He said that it was her choice, and they asked her if she wanted them to do the procedure, or to just end it and let her go peacefully, and she opted to do the procedure. Had my uncle not been right next to her with tears in his eyes, she would have chosen a different fate, but she chose to live a little longer.

All day long I just kept thinking about how much I wanted the suffering to end for her; *release is peace* I kept thinking to myself as the day went on, and little did I know, my wishes and prayers were going to be answered quicker than I had thought. When I got home from school, I stood by my somehow emotionally stable dad for the remainder of the day simply to get away from my own thoughts. The night rolled around, and like deja vu, we got a phone call from my uncle in the midst of watching the Yankees game. My dad once again left with tears in his eyes, and I called any friend or relative I could think of just to talk about it and numb the hysteria that was going on in my mind. I fell in and out of consciousness all night long, my mind and heart racing with fear. I ended up waking up at around 8:30 on Friday morning. I went downstairs, woke up my stepmom and asked her why no one had woken us up for school. She had told us that our father had gotten home from the hospital at 4 a.m. and that he desperately needed sleep. I knew what was about to come next, but it still hit me like a ton of bricks when the words came out of her mouth. "Grandma passed away last night." I did not know how to react, so my first instinct was to go to school just to get my mind off of it. It was a weird day, a day of getting hugs from all my friends that I had told prior to going into school, and asking all of my teachers to cut me some slack while I was staring into space and thinking about the news that I had received that morning. The relieving feeling of the ninth period bell was finally there, this time more relieving than ever. When I got home from school, I had asked my dad to take me through what happened the night before. He said when he went to the hospital, the doctor spoke to both him and my uncle and said that nothing they were doing was working, her heart will not be able to take all of the things that they are giving her, and that she could have until the middle of the night or the middle of the next day at most. After about an hour of keeping my emotionally unstable uncle company, they both decided to go back home and get some rest. He then said he got a call at midnight, it was once again my uncle. He said that my grandma's vital numbers were rapidly going down, and that they wanted them to be there in case anything happened. When my dad was about half way to the hospital, my uncle called again and said the hospital called to say they got everything under control. My dad decided to go back home and try to go back to sleep again. The second he laid down at about 1:30 a.m., he got one last call from my uncle. This time, he said all choked up and crying hysterically, "John, I think you're going to want to come here right now." My dad had replied, "Why? What's wrong?" and again my uncle said, "I think you're going to want to come here right now." When my dad got to the hospital, Grandma was gone. Her heart had given out from all the things that were being done to her, and just like that, it was over.

It was now Saturday, September 23rd, the day of the wake. It was a crisp day that seemed much colder and darker than it actually was. My family was at the funeral home an hour before the wake began, just to be able to mourn together as a family, and see my grandma in the casket for the first time. It once again seemed like everyone in my family except for me was crying. As I walked into the room with my dad, my brother, and my uncle, I took a long look around. There was a television set that was showing a slide show of my grandma from when she was a child, up until the present day. I noticed that there were black and white photos of her as a baby, and pictures of her when she was in her senior year of high school. She was beautiful; she had actually modeled from when she was in late high school up until when she had my father. As the pictures went on, I began to see pictures of her and my dad when he was just a baby, then of him when he was in high school, then when he was married to my mother, then I saw her in pictures with me when I was less than two years old, and some more when I was about fifteen. She looked so happy, full of life; the permanent smile that was imprinted on her face was there in every single picture. I stared at the television until I saw each picture at least three times. After that, it was then time to go up to the casket and say hello to her. She looked like a wax sculpture; she had a blonde wig on that I had seen her wear before when we were at her house to visit. She definitely looked better than the last time I saw her. It was relieving to see no tubes, no needles, no oxygen tanks preventing her from speaking to me. She had rosary beads grasped in her hands, and I placed a small metal angel on her shoulder. The casket would be closed for the wakes, as she wished, and act one began. For two and a half hours I walked around hugging and kissing family members that I had not seen since I was a baby; and even some people who I had never seen before. Friends from school came to pay their condolences, as well as friends of my dad and uncle. We left the funeral home at about 9:45 p.m.—all of us exhausted and desperately needing to just lie down, rest, and somehow get through this.

I spent all night dreading the day that would follow, and didn't get any sleep. I stared at my ceiling as the hours passed, and as soon as the sun rose the next morning, the stomachache, the pain in my chest, the overall feeling of going to a funeral began. The first stop was the funeral home to say our final goodbyes. When I arrived there with my family, we went up to the casket one last time. There she was again, looking as calm and nice as always, this time there were more things in her coffin. Pictures of my dad, my uncle James, and my other uncle Thomas, who died a few years before I was born, were all in her arms. There were also pictures of her and my great aunt Mary. It was not easy to go up there and say goodbye to my grandmother who I knew couldn't answer me, but I spent the final seconds up there to just thank her and send her my love. I still had been questioning myself as to why I was not crying, but that all changed as soon as we got to the church. The first thing I saw was a man who was apparently a member of my family whom I had never seen before. He was wearing a plaid shirt and a kilt and was holding bagpipes. He began to play *Amazing Grace* on his bagpipes, as four men unloaded my grandma in the casket from the car, and at that very moment, the floodgates in my eyes burst wide open. I finally blended in with the rest of my family who was doing the same thing that I was, and we all sat down in the pew and began mass. My grandma's casket was placed right in the middle of the aisle, and I sat in the front row with my father, my brother, and my uncle, aunt and stepmom. Forty-five minutes of tears and readings from the bible finally ended, in what felt like forever. It was time for the rollercoaster to finally come to an end, as we took the trip to the cemetery. The ceremony went relatively quick surprisingly. There was one last goodbye as everyone placed their rose on the platform where her casket would be, and it was unexpectedly the quickest of them all. After the ceremony at the cemetery, the whole family had lunch at the Irish Coffee Pub. For the first time in months, the atmosphere was relaxed, and every member of my family was joyous and happy. We were all there for about four hours until finally going home at about five o'clock.

After a long day, I sat on my couch with my dad. There was not too much talking going on, just a lot of thoughts. I began to think about my grandmother, reflecting on the good times we had. I thought about all the times she would babysit when I was little, all the times she took my brother and me out to dinner, and all the nights we slept over her house. It finally hit me that I would never have those moments again, and before I knew it, the entire weeks' worth of tears began to pour out of my disheartened face. I just wanted to see her once more, give her one last hug and say goodbye the right way. I wanted to just see a healthy her, with a full head of hair and a lot of life in her. The thought of never seeing her again finally set in, but at the same time it was consolatory, because I knew that the pain was finally over.

Reflecting upon it now, it taught me a lot about life. It taught me that everything happens for a reason, and that it will always work out in the end. My grandmother was the greatest and strongest person I knew. She sat on a hospital bed fearless and laughed in the face of death. She dared her disease to try and get her down and mocked it as it got increasingly worse over time. But through all the pain she dealt with and despite all the suffering she went through over the past ten months, she never broke her smile, and it ended just how she would have wanted: her going peacefully without pain and her family coming together to get through it as one.

Chapter 32

DIAGNOSIS

By: Cassidy Latham

You can't make cancer sound beautiful. Dying isn't an art.

That's all you can manage to say. Because it's midnight and your throat is knotted. Your eyes burn red and you can't bear to look in the mirror.

You're sitting at a red light with your cousin on the way home from the hospital. And he's not sure what to do when you start crying. And all that you can see is her shaking, and her eyes flickering helplessly, and the IV pulsing morphine beneath her ghostly skin. And as of 2:06 a.m., you'll never see her again.

The night is cruel. When it's pitch black and all hope has gone with the casket spread. They expect your emptiness to be filled with the skin-deep sorrows of cold apologies.

Sometimes memories are cruel. Sometimes emotions are uncontrollable. Sometimes you follow a cherry wood casket into a church. Your chest is hyperventilating, and you keep your eyes on the cross, so you don't have to look anybody in the eye. And here you sit, and there she lies. Cancer has stolen another away.

Her smile's long gone. She was taken from your heart and put in the ground. And she won't be the only one that cancer will take from you. And she can never give you another birthday card, or come to your school concert and hug you afterword. She can't show off about you to her neighbors, or give you just one last smile.

And the white rose you put on her casket will die, too.

You'd sit at the kitchen table. She'd read your favorite book, and the safety of her words filled you with warmth. It's all fun and games when you're three years old, isn't it? But you're not three years old anymore. So you held her hand. And the tears streamed down your face, and you got home that night and screamed at the top of your lungs. And you bit your tongue so hard you tasted blood. You couldn't sleep so you wrapped yourself in her blanket and took a deep breath. It still smells like her. And maybe that moment you breathed in, she breathed out. Breathed out the never ending thirst, the empty stomach, the IVs and the coughing. The coughing that echoes in your mind every single night.

And the memories of your best friend are fading. And you blink too long and they're gone. And she's gone, and you're empty. Your heart aches. You can't see straight.

Sometimes the end is cruel. The gasps for breath. The bony back.

But there's nothing you can do, right? So the priest walks in and the oxygen comes out. And they encircle her bed and manage some sort of goodbye. And her suffering is finally over. So are her witty little remarks and warm hellos. And with time, the memories of you and her rolling cookies at the kitchen table will fade. And you'll grab them, snatching balloons that have begun drifting up into the clouds. Sometimes we don't catch them in time.

Life goes on. Cry yourself to sleep. Wake up. Dry mouth, wet eyes, clutching her blanket. Pretend it was a dream; a nightmare.

No single person has ever been diagnosed with cancer. No single person has ever been diagnosed with the five days a week of radiation, endless chemotherapy, and a hospital room with a clock that's too fast. Because when we crowded around my grandma, on the last night I would hear her breathe, I came upon the simple realization that shook my perspective on life itself. The moment the spot was found on her lung, we were all diagnosed with cancer.

Made in the USA
San Bernardino, CA
11 January 2018